Oafs of Office ... and Other
Outlandish Behavior!

President Jimmy Carter filed a detailed report of his sighting of a UFO over Leary, Georgia, in 1969. . . . The truth is out there, and so are some of our presidents!

Ulysses S. Grant not only was infamous for his alcohol addiction, he became addicted to cocaine while under treatment for throat cancer.

"Richard Nixon is a no-good lying bastard. He can lie out of both sides of his mouth at the same time and if he ever caught himself telling the truth, he'd lie just to keep his hand in." —Harry S Truman on Richard Nixon

During a 1996 trip to Costa Rica, President Bill Clinton stopped at the Braulio Carrillo National Park, a government-protected rain forest, and said in a speech, "We destroy these resources at our own peril" . . . right after his staff bulldozed and paved a 350-foot strip of that forest to make it easier for him to reach the speaking platform.

As a young law student at Duke University, Richard Nixon was reprimanded after being caught breaking into the dean's office. Some people just don't learn. . . .

In 1995, during the Bob Hope Golf Classic, Bill Clinton scored 100, Gerald Ford hit a spectator with a ball, and George Bush struck two—one of the wounded onlookers required ten stitches on her nose.

ALL TRUE. ALL RECORDED IN THE PUBLIC RECORD.
AND ALL WE NEED TO KNOW TO WONDER . . .
WHAT'S GONNA HAPPEN NEXT!

Also by Leland H. Gregory III

PRESUMED IGNORANT!

GREAT GOVERNMENT GOOFS!

Presidential

Indiscretions

Leland H. Gregory III

A DELL TRADE PAPERBACK

A DELL TRADE PAPERBACK

Published by
Dell Publishing
a division of Random House, Inc.
1540 Broadway
New York, New York 10036

Library of Congress Cataloging in Publication Data
Gregory, Leland.
    Presidential indiscretions / Leland H. Gregory III.
        p.   cm.
    ISBN 0-440-50792-8
    1. Presidents—United States—Biography—Anecdotes.   2. Presidents—United States—Humor.   I. Title.
    E176.1 .L34 1999
    973'.09'9—dc21   98-53045
                        CIP

Original art by Daniel Lynch

Printed in the United States of America

Published simultaneously in Canada

June 1999

10   9   8   7   6   5   4   3   2   1

BVG

This book is dedicated to my wife, Gloria, for her encouragement, love, understanding, and friendship. I love you and I love the way you love our son.

Acknowledgments

First and foremost I would like to acknowledge the accomplishments of the forty-one men who have served as president of the United States—some great, some not so great, some pretty stinky. I would also like to thank the voting public, myself included, who elected these particular fellows—it made my job a lot easier.

I would like to thank my wife, Gloria Gregory, for her patience and love. We have been together roughly the equivalent of three presidential terms and she hasn't impeached me yet.

I would also like to thank Jonathon Lazear, all the people at the Lazear Agency, as well as my editor at Dell, Kathleen Jayes.

I pray Heaven to bestow the best of blessings on this house and all that shall hereafter inhabit it. May none but honest and wise men ever rule under this roof.

—President John Adams, second president of the United States, in 1800, written the day after he moved into the new White House

Nice idea there, John, but mostly it's been filled with . . .

Presidential

Indiscretions

The Cast—In Order of Appearance

1. **George Washington,** Federalist. Virginia, 1789–97
2. **John Adams,** Federalist. Massachusetts, 1797–1801
3. **Thomas Jefferson,** D. Virginia, 1801–09
4. **James Madison,** D. Virginia, 1809–17
5. **James Monroe,** D. Virginia, 1817–25
6. **John Quincy Adams,** D. Massachusetts, 1825–29
7. **Andrew Jackson,** D. Tennessee, 1829–37
8. **Martin Van Buren,** D. New York, 1837–41
9. **William Henry Harrison,** Whig. Ohio, 1841
10. **John Tyler,** Whig. Virginia, 1841–45
11. **James Knox Polk,** D. Tennessee, 1845–49
12. **Zachary Taylor,** Whig. Kentucky, 1849–50
13. **Millard Fillmore,** Whig. New York, 1850–53
14. **Franklin Pierce,** D. New Hampshire, 1853–57
15. **James Buchanan,** D. Pennsylvania, 1857–61
16. **Abraham Lincoln,** R. Illinois, 1861–65
17. **Andrew Johnson,** R. Tennessee, 1865–69
18. **Ulysses Simpson Grant,** R. Ohio, 1869–77
19. **Rutherford Birchard Hayes,** R. Ohio, 1877–81
20. **James Abram Garfield,** R. Ohio, 1881
21. **Chester Alan Arthur,** R. New York, 1881–85
*22. **Grover Cleveland,** D. New York, 1885–89, 1893–97
23. **Benjamin Harrison,** R. Indiana, 1889–93
24. **William McKinley,** R. Ohio, 1897–1901
25. **Theodore Roosevelt,** R. New York, 1901–09
26. **William Howard Taft,** R. Ohio, 1909–13

27. Woodrow Wilson, D. New Jersey, 1913–21

28. Warren Gamaliel Harding, R. Ohio, 1921–23

29. Calvin Coolidge, R. Massachusetts, 1923–29

30. Herbert Hoover, R. California, 1929–33

31. Franklin Delano Roosevelt, D. New York, 1933–45

32. Harry S Truman, D. Missouri, 1945–53

33. Dwight David Eisenhower, R. Kansas, 1953–61

34. John Fitzgerald Kennedy, D. Massachusetts, 1961–63

35. Lyndon Baines Johnson, D. Texas, 1963–69

36. Richard Milhous Nixon, R. California, 1969–74

37. Gerald Rudolph Ford, R. Michigan, 1974–77

38. James Earl Carter, D. Georgia, 1977–81

39. Ronald Wilson Reagan, R. California, 1981–89

40. George Herbert Walker Bush, R. Texas, 1989–93

41. William Jefferson Clinton, D. Arkansas, 1993–

*Grover Cleveland is the only president to have been elected in nonconsecutive years.

Deep Washington Roots

Relatively speaking, the king of all kinfolk was Franklin D. Roosevelt, who was related by blood or marriage to eleven other presidents: John Adams, John Quincy Adams, Ulysses S. Grant, William Henry Harrison, Benjamin Harrison, James Madison, Theodore Roosevelt, William Howard Taft, John Taylor, Martin Van Buren, and George Washington.

He was also a seventh cousin once removed of British leader Winston Churchill and a second cousin seven times removed of Queen Elizabeth II. He was even related to his wife, Eleanor Roosevelt: She was his fifth cousin once removed. In fact, Eleanor Roosevelt's maiden name was Eleanor Roosevelt, which means that this marriage was more than just a convenience . . . it saved young Eleanor a lot of money. She didn't have to have anything remonogrammed.

The real father of our country: John Tyler was the father of fifteen children. His last child, Pearl, was born when Tyler was past his seventieth birthday.

Lost in the Translation

John F. Kennedy took a historic trip to West Berlin during the crisis that divided that city. While he was there he spoke four words that would ring throughout the world, "Ich bin ein Berliner." Kennedy wanted to assure the people of Berlin that he supported their cause of freedom—even though their nation was now divided. His quote is:

All free men, wherever they may live, are citizens of Berlin, and, therefore, as a free man, I take pride in the words "Ich bin ein Berliner."

He had hoped to say "I am a Berliner." Unfortunately, "Ich bin ein Berliner" literally translates into "I am a jelly doughnut." The crowd applauded appreciatively, either because they understood what Kennedy was trying to say—or they loved a good pastry.

"Elevate them guns a little lower!" —President Andrew Jackson, in 1815, at the battle of Mobile, Alabama

Just Horsing Around

In 1853 President Franklin Pierce, widely known for his losing battle with the bottle, was arrested in Washington, D.C., after accidentally running down an elderly lady, Mrs. Nathan Lewis, with his horse. Mrs. Lewis wasn't injured but Constable Stanley Edelin placed the president in custody. No matter what kind of executive privileges the president has, the U.S. Constitution doesn't give the president immunity from arrest. Mrs. Lewis was in stable condition, Pierce's horse was placed in a stable, and the president's term of office was unstable at best.

"This will be the commencement of the decline of my reputation." —George Washington, after learning that the Continental Congress had unanimously elected him as its choice as commander-in-chief of the Continental Army in 1775

Let's Focus, People

Focus groups are an important part of any political campaign these days. A select group of people are chosen, and their input and attitudes are measured, which, in turn, helps the candidate and his staff figure out what the voters might like. During the 1996 presidential campaign, Republican presidential hopeful Bob Dole asked a focus group to name animals they associated with Republican presidential candidates. With Phil Gramm they associated ferrets, foxes, hyenas, and weasels; Pat Buchanan was aligned with badgers, pit bulls, and wolverines; and Bob Dole himself was paired with chameleons, draft horses, kangaroos, mules, and tortoises.

With his first profession being that of a tailor, President Andrew Johnson let it be known that he only wore tailor-made suits—made, that is, by himself.

Harding's Presidency
Was for the Dogs

Granted, Warren G. Harding is considered one of America's worst presidents; his cabinet was racked with corruption and as president he accomplished few things worth mentioning. However, while he may not have been the American voters' best choice, he does earn the title "Dog's Best Friend." In fact, he was the first chief executive to give a dog a presidential pardon. One morning Harding read a newspaper article about a dog in Pennsylvania that was going to be put to sleep because it had been brought into the country illegally. Harding, who loved dogs, quickly wrote a letter to the governor of Pennsylvania demanding that the termination be terminated. The governor, not wanting to go against an executive order, saw to it that the dog was taken off death row and set free. I suppose every dog has his day—even a dog of a president.

While a high school student in the early 1930s, Richard Nixon worked for two summers as a barker for the wheel-of-chance at the Slippery Gulch Rodeo in Prescott, Arizona.

Playing Ketchup

In 1981 a woman concerned over the plight of the economy, both hers and America's in general, sat down and wrote a letter to President Ronald Reagan. She explained in the letter that as a mother of four she was having a difficult time feeding her children on the reduced food stamps program. The woman knew full well she would probably receive a form letter explaining Reagan's position on the matter—but she didn't expect the kind of form letter she received. Someone at the White House thought her letter was a request for a recipe and forwarded it to the First Lady's office. Nancy Reagan quickly responded to the woman with a Reagan family favorite, crabmeat and asparagus casserole, costing about twenty dollars to prepare.

This was at a time when, as the *New York Times* wrote, "the Reagan administration was in the midst of trying to declare ketchup a vegetable and lines of the hungry were forming to pick up surplus cheese." President Reagan claimed the situation caused him "considerable embarrassment" and that he would look into the matter. So how did the Reagan administration rectify the situation? Well, thereafter, when a request was sent to the White House, the First Lady's office mailed out one of Ronald Reagan's favorite recipes: macaroni and cheese. And during the early eighties, if you put ketchup on it, you would have had a meal consisting of three of the four food groups.

Abraham Lincoln suffered from chronic constipation.

Presidents on the Presidency

We know it's considered one of the most powerful positions in the world—but what have the presidents really thought about their job?

"The four most miserable years of my life were my four years in the Presidency." —John Quincy Adams

"It is hell! No other word can describe it."
   —Warren Harding, on the presidency

"I'll be damned if I am not getting tired of this. It seems to be the profession of a President simply to hear other people talk."
   —William Howard Taft

"I knew this job would be too much for me."
   —President Warren G. Harding

"My God! What is there in this place that a man should ever want to get in?" —James Garfield, on life in the White House

All the Way with LBJ. The initials "LBJ" don't just stand for Lyndon Baines Johnson. They actually stand for every member of the Johnson family: Lady Bird Johnson, his wife; their daughters, Lynda Bird Johnson and Luci Baines Johnson; and the family dog, Little Beagle Johnson.

Dating by Carbon Dating

In May 1996, the National Geographic Society drew long lines in Washington, D.C., with its exhibit of a five-hundred-year-old mummy. The mummy was of a sacrificed teenage Inca girl and was recovered in remarkable condition from the top of a Peruvian volcano. At a Democratic Party fund-raiser Senator Joseph Lieberman of Connecticut joked: "In high school, she dated Bob Dole." This got a resounding wave of laughter and applause from the crowd.

When it was President Clinton's turn to speak at the fund-raiser, he remarked: "I don't know if you've seen that mummy. But, you know, if I were a single man, I might ask that mummy out. That's a good-looking mummy." The author is surprised that independent counsel Kenneth Starr didn't subpoena the mummy—but then, she would probably have kept her testimony under wraps.

"I'm not trying to compare myself with Roosevelt, but he couldn't walk either." —The wheelchair-bound George Wallace, during his 1976 presidential campaign

Tubby's Tub

Someone's got to have the distinction of being the heaviest president, and that honor goes to William Howard Taft. Taft varied in weight from 300 to more than 350 pounds (when he was depressed). One day, William Howard Taft sat down in the presidential bathtub to soak off the stress of the day—and stayed there for longer than he had anticipated. He was stuck. It was an embarrassing thing to have happen, and as soon as he was rescued, he ordered an enormous personalized tub for himself. The J. L. Mott Iron Works made the tub to Taft's specifications and installed it in the White House. When it was being delivered, four White House staffers had their photograph taken—all four men fit comfortably inside the new tub.

At birth, Richard Nixon weighed eleven pounds.

Two Heads of State Are Better than One

Has the United States ever had more than one president in power at the same time? Yes, actually. The presidential race between Rutherford B. Hayes and Samuel Tilden was highly contested. Tilden had beaten Hayes by more than 250,000 popular votes but Hayes won the presidency with one controversial electoral vote. There was talk of Tilden's group forcibly taking over the White House—it was a very unnerving time, especially for Hayes. While dining at the White House with President Ulysses S. Grant on the eve of the scheduled inauguration, Grant, Hayes, and Chief Justice Morrison B. Waite quietly excused themselves and went into the Red Room together, where Hayes took the oath of office to forestall any attempted coups. Therefore, technically, both Grant and Hayes were simultaneously president of the United States. The next day, on the east steps of the Capitol building, Hayes officially was administered the oath of office. But even if you combine Grant and Hayes—it still would make for one lousy president.

When Andrew Jackson left the presidency at age seventy he had only ninety dollars in cash to his name.

They Paved Paradise and Put Up a Photo Op

During a trip to Costa Rica in the spring of 1996, President Bill Clinton stopped off at the Braulio Carrillo National Park—a government-protected rain forest—to give a speech about environmental protection and preservation. His address included the line "We destroy these resources at our own peril." Too bad Bill's staff didn't agree. Clinton's people thought the speaking platform was too far from the road, especially since the President was on crutches at the time. They decided to bulldoze and pave with asphalt a 350-foot path for him—right through the rain forest. Later a White House staffer tried to put a good spin on it: "The Costa Ricans were eager to pave the walkway for the President. They seemed to understand how important a photo op this was for us." Sounds like an example of not being able to see the trees for the forest. Any more photo ops like this and we won't be able to see the trees *or* the forest.

**In his hometown of Abilene, Kansas, kids used to call
Dwight David Eisenhower "Ugly Ike."**

A Gay Ol' Tale

The truth may never come out of the closet on this one—there might not have been a closet to come out of. It's the story of two men—James Buchanan and William Rufus De Vane King. One later became the fifteenth president of the United States, the other vice president under Franklin Pierce. But when they first met each other while serving as members of Congress they became immediately inseparable. It has been rumored for years that Buchanan and King were a "couple" but it's never been proven. Buchanan was, however, the only bachelor ever elected president—he never married and was never seen with another woman after his fiancée, Anne Coleman, died suddenly of mysterious causes fifteen years before Buchanan joined the Senate. What is known is that Buchanan and King were commonly referred to by other members of Congress as "Mr. Buchanan and his wife" and "Miss Nancy and Aunt Fancy."

"I watch a lot of baseball on radio." —President Gerald Ford, on ABC-TV's *Monday Night Baseball*, 1978, as quoted in Bob Chieger's *Voices of Baseball*

A Flea-Bitten Administration

It's true, Warren G. Harding loved dogs. We know he gave a presidential pardon to a dog that saved the mongrel's life. He also made sure his beloved dog Laddie Boy was assigned Dog License #1. On Laddie Boy's birthday, Harding threw a big party at the White House in his honor—complete with a cake made of layered dog biscuits covered with frosting. I hope that treat was meant only for the dogs.

James Buchanan had the habit of closing one eye in order to see—he was nearsighted in one eye and farsighted in the other.

Run Silent Run Deep

Even though Theodore Roosevelt was probably the most athletic, sports-minded, and outdoorsy of all the presidents, "Silent Cal" Coolidge, who took office in 1923, liked the great outdoors, too. He enjoyed fishing, but he wasn't a "hands-on" fisherman—he was more like a "gloves-on" fisherman. Coolidge always wore gloves when he fished. He even ordered Secret Service agents to both bait his line and take off any fish he might have hooked. The agents complained bitterly about being Coolidge's "bait-boys." They were, after all, supposed to protect the president's life, not his fish.

James A. Garfield experienced recurring nightmares in which he was lost in a primeval forest—completely naked.

Bully or
Just Plain Bull?

If there's one thing Teddy Roosevelt is remembered for, other than saying "Bully," it's his legendary ride up San Juan Hill. Teddy Roosevelt and the Rough Riders' charge is credited for turning the tide of the Spanish-American War. The image of hundreds of men on horseback, led by a barrel-chested Teddy Roosevelt, sword in hand, yelling "charge" at the top of his lungs, is a pretty impressive image, to be sure. But it's not the way it really happened. The First Regiment of U.S. Cavalry Volunteers organized by Theodore Roosevelt and nicknamed "the Rough Riders" was made up of 1,000 men—mostly friends of Roosevelt's: cowboys, college athletes, miners, law-enforcement officials, and Harvard bluebloods. They trained for two months in Texas before shipping off to Cuba.

But when it came time to board the ships, there was only enough room on board for 560 men and certainly no room for their 1,200 horses and pack mules. So the legendary charge up San Juan Hill was made mainly on foot. Here's another kick in the legendary pants. Theodore Roosevelt didn't lead the charge. Colonel Leonard Wood was in command of that attack. So, let's picture the real event. Approximately 600 men on foot running up a hill in Cuba led by someone named Wood, not Roosevelt. After the battle, the Rough Riders renamed themselves "Wood's Weary Walkers." The version of the story that we've come to know and love was invented by Roosevelt during his presidential campaign. Teddy may have been tough as a bull moose—but it was bull@!#! that he was good at.

After being elected president, Jimmy Carter began parting his hair on the left, instead of the right.

So Quiet You Could Hear a Pen Drop

In order to persuade the North Vietnamese to give up communism and embrace "the American Way," thousands of "Democracy Kits" were dropped over North Vietnam in 1972. The kits contained, among other things, pen-and-pencil sets, decorated with the presidential seal and the signature of Richard Nixon. Why did the American military decide to drop pen-and-pencil sets over North Vietnam? The sets were originally designed to be given to Nixon's generous political contributors; the ones dropped over North Vietnam had been leftovers. Nixon probably used the donation of pen-and-pencil sets as a tax write-off.

**Franklin D. Roosevelt had "Stolen from the White House"
printed on the cover of all the White House matchbooks.**

Show Me the Money!!!

Money makes the world go around—especially the world of politics. During the 1996 presidential elections some interesting financial contributions rolled into the various camps. President Clinton's reelection campaign received a check from the "Hemp Growers of America" in the amount of $100. Pat Buchanan's campaign also received a $100 check, this one from "Abortionists for Buchanan." Each check was clearly labeled with the group's name and both checks were cashed. The thing is, neither group really exists except in the mind of filmmaker Michael Moore (best known for the satirical documentary on General Motors, *Roger and Me*). Moore bragged that the fictitious "Hemp Growers of America" group even got two thank-you notes from the Clinton camp. Moore's little joke ended there—for the simple reason that Bob Dole and Ross Perot obviously watch their money more carefully. Dole's staff returned a $100 check from "Satan Worshipers for Dole." And Perot sent back a check for $100 from the group "Pedophiles for Free Trade."

"This is still the greatest country in the world, if we just steel our wills and lose our minds." —President Bill Clinton

Mother Knows Best

At age fourteen, George Washington received word from his half brother Lawrence that Captain Green of the British Royal Navy was looking to bring aboard a new midshipman. Washington knew a spot in His Majesty's Navy would mean a lifetime of adventure as well as a wonderful career. George told his half brother that he was very interested in the appointment but he had to get the approval of his mother first. Mary Washington, who ruled over George most of his life, seriously considered the plan and at one point nearly gave George her blessing. But, after some soul-searching, Mary decided that George should stay with her and not dedicate his life to the sea. We should all be thankful for Mary Washington's decision because had she allowed George to take that appointment in 1746, he would have been fighting on the side of the British during the American Revolution!

During World War II, President Franklin D. Roosevelt's wheelchair was equipped with a gas mask.

Pay No Attention to the
Woman Behind the Napkin

President William McKinley always arranged to have his wife, Ida McKinley, seated next to him at any official function. He didn't do it out of affection or chivalry; he did it in case he needed to throw a handkerchief or napkin over her face. Ida McKinley was left an epileptic after a traumatic childbirth experience delivering her daughter, Ida. Even though she was prone to seizures, the president's wife insisted on attending ceremonies and dinners with her husband. When one of her seizures struck, leaving Ida's face horribly contorted, the president would casually drape a handkerchief over her face until she recovered.

**President Theodore Roosevelt's family kept a
one-legged chicken in the White House as a pet.**

You Thought Mary Todd Lincoln Was Strange!

Just sixty days before Franklin Pierce's presidential inauguration took place, his eleven-year-old son, Benny, was killed in a railway accident. Franklin Pierce briefly discussed forgoing his inauguration but his wife, Jane Pierce, insisted that Benny was killed so that Franklin wouldn't have any distractions when he took over as president. She saw Benny's death as a divine act from God. Once Franklin Pierce took over the reins of government, Jane declined to participate in any White House function, no matter how small or how large, and spent most of her time locked in her room writing letters to her dead son.

"The Internet is a great way to get on the net."
—Former Republican presidential candidate Bob Dole

A Mere Drop in the Bucket

If Clinton can pave the way in the rain forest for a photo op, then his Vice President can make sure the tide rises during his. When Vice President Al Gore visited Denver, Colorado, in March 1996, he was set to give a speech and have a media photo op in front of the South Platte River. Too bad the water was so low at that point. Enter Hamlet "Chips" Barry III, chief of the city's water department, to the rescue. Barry ordered 96 million gallons of water released into the river to make it look more appealing as a backdrop for Gore photos. The *Rocky Mountain News* reported the water was worth $59,000 and could have supplied nearly 300 families for a year. "I can defend it," Barry said. "When you have the river being showcased, you want it to look good." Too bad he couldn't do anything about Al.

Franklin D. Roosevelt was forced by his mother to wear dresses until the age of five.

Don't Leave Home Without It

Michael Robinson, who worked at a restaurant in Americus, Georgia, obtained a credit card number from a customer and went on a brief buying spree in July 1997. His first stop was a music store where he purchased $45.27 worth of compact discs and charged it to the stolen credit card account. Imagine his surprise when he was arrested soon thereafter by Secret Service agents. The credit card number he'd stolen was that of former president Jimmy Carter!

While president of the United States, Ulysses S. Grant had his horse and carriage impounded and he himself was arrested for speeding on a Washington street.

It Just Doesn't Add Up

The lawsuits the Clinton administration has been hit with are nothing new—presidents have been sued throughout time for a variety of reasons. One case, *Lorenzo Grier* v. *United States of America,* claimed that President Ronald Reagan was guilty of . . . well, you'll see:

> Appellant alleged that former President Ronald Reagan did not respond when Appellant invented the multiplication tables and sent them to the White House, but instead stole Appellant's invention and implemented it in the public schools. Appellant sought damages of $900 billion for fraud, breach of contract and discrimination.

Strangely enough, in July 1995, the United States District Court in Alexandria, Virginia, dismissed the case as having no legal basis. Apparently the sum of Grier's argument wasn't equal to the total of his imagination.

During his childhood and into his teens, Andrew Jackson suffered from habitual slobbering. He eventually overcame this disability.

Another Harding Dog Tail— Eh, Tale

When President Warren G. Harding died, the Newsboys Association of America, of which Harding was also president, decided to pay homage to their fallen leader. They arranged to build a statue of Harding's beloved dog Laddie Boy as a tribute to their fallen leader. In order to raise money for the statue, the Newsboys Association requested that each newspaper boy in America donate one penny. Soon 103 pounds of pennies were collected. This horde of pennies was melted down to provide the bronze for the statue. Even though the Harding administration left no lasting impression on the United States, his love of dogs did. The statue of Laddie Boy can still be seen at the Smithsonian Institution.

**"[He's an] 85-year-old chain-smoking Communist dwarf."
—Patrick Buchanan during his 1992 presidential campaign on Chinese leader Deng Xiaoping**

A Day in the Life

David Rice Atchison. Not the most familiar name in the world. Less known, even, than say, Millard Fillmore. But David Rice Atchison should be in the history books along with all the other presidents of the United States. Why? Because technically, David Rice Atchison was president of the United States—if only for one day. What happened was James K. Polk was to end his presidency at noon on March 4, 1849, and Zachary Taylor was scheduled to take the presidential oath of office that same day. But March 4 fell on a Sunday. Taylor didn't think it proper to take the oath of office on that day and decided Monday, March 5, would do much better.

That meant from noon on March 4, 1849, when Polk's term expired, until noon of March 5, when Taylor would be sworn in, the United States would be without a president. The law dictates that "in case of the removal, death, resignation or disability of both the President and Vice President of the United States, the President of the Senate Pro Tempore shall act as President." And the President of the Senate Pro Tempore at the time was—you got it, David Rice Atchison. Atchison was never sworn in, never lived at the White House, and didn't know he had been president for a day until years later. He died in 1886 and his home state, Missouri, erected a monument in his honor with the legend: "David Rice Atchison. President of the U.S. for one day. Lawyer, statesman and jurist."

He has still been denied his place among the other presidents of the United States—which is just as well, since people are generally known by the company they keep.

**Republican Harold Stassen sought the presidential
nomination unsuccessfully nine times between
1944 and 1992.**

Testing—One, Two . . .

According to a Federal Protective Service report cited in the *Washington Times*, staff and volunteers of the 1993 Clinton inaugural gala took off with $154,000 worth of electronic equipment used during the festivities.

"In America, anyone can become president. That's one of the risks you take."—Adlai Stevenson, Democratic presidential nominee against Dwight D. Eisenhower

Take Me to Your Leader

Jimmy Carter is credited with a number of things: bringing together the leaders of Saudi Arabia and Egypt; giving a heartfelt interview for *Playboy*; and being one of only two one-term presidents in recent history. (Bush was the other). He's also known for being the only president to have seen an unidentified flying object, or UFO. About one year before he was elected governor of Georgia, Jimmy Carter filed a detailed report of his sighting of a UFO over Leary, Georgia, on the evening of January 6, 1969. He was attending a meeting of the Lions Club and was standing outdoors with ten other members waiting for the meeting to begin. Around 7:30 P.M., Carter and the other men saw a distinctly outlined light in the sky. Carter said it appeared "bluish at first—then reddish—but not solid . . . It appeared as bright as the moon" and seemed to "move toward us from a distance, stop, move partially away, return, then depart." He also wrote in the "sighting report" for the International UFO Bureau in Oklahoma City that he had observed the object for nearly twelve minutes, that it was completely silent and was approximately nine hundred yards away. "I'll never make fun of people who say they've seen unidentified objects in the sky," Carter said. The truth is out there—and so are some of our presidents.

"A barbed-wire enema." —Presidential candidate
Patrick Buchanan in 1992, defining how the media
reacted to his campaign platform

The Wilson Follies

Woodrow Wilson didn't always dream of becoming the president of the United States. As a college student he actually had ambitions for the stage. Eventually, he gave up the theatrical life for one with nearly as much drama, but he never lost his first love. As president, he would still attend the theater. He particularly liked vaudeville, and when he returned to the White House after his outings, he would entertain his family by mimicking the tap dancers and singers he had seen earlier. It makes sense—most presidents have to do a little sidestepping now and then.

When John F. Kennedy was assassinated in Dallas in 1963, it was not a federal felony to kill a president of the United States.

Look What Developed

Abraham Lincoln, among his other contributions, was the first president to be photographed at his inauguration. In a classic "Lincoln Weirdness," one photo shows Lincoln standing near the man whose name will forever be associated with his—John Wilkes Booth.

While under treatment for cancer of the throat, Ulysses S. Grant admitted he had become addicted to cocaine.

Dog Day Afternoon

Gerald Ford brought with him to the White House a golden retriever named Liberty. Liberty was usually kept in a kennel on the ground floor of the White House but during her pregnancy she was moved to a room on the third floor, closer to her trainer. One evening the trainer had to leave the White House and President Ford offered to keep the dog in his bedroom in case she needed him. "Mr. President, she's no trouble at all," said the trainer. "If she wants to go out, she'll come and lick your face."

At approximately three o'clock in the morning, President Ford was awoken by Liberty's wet tongue lapping at his face. Ford put on his robe and slippers, took the elevator to the ground floor, and walked out onto the White House lawn with Liberty. Once Liberty had relieved herself, the president headed inside to go back to bed. One problem: When he pushed the button on the elevator, nothing happened. The elevator had been shut off for the night. The president led Liberty up the stairs. When they got to the door of the presidential family living quarters, Ford found it locked. So he walked down to the second floor and tried that door— no luck there either. Here's the most powerful man in the free world, wearing pajamas and slippers, walking around with a pregnant dog on a leash, and he can't even get back into his own bedroom.

Once this thought occurred to Ford he became angry and started pounding on the walls. Within seconds the White House security staff jumped into action: Lights came on, shouting was heard, doors flew open, and Ford was suddenly surrounded by Secret Service agents, guns drawn, blood in their eyes. When they realized they had surrounded the president of the United States and his pregnant dog, they were, to say the least, embarrassed. Gerald "Mr. Nice Guy" Ford calmed the agents down, told them not to worry, and asked if he could go to bed. Liberty gave birth to nine puppies in the White House days after the lockout. She and her little puppies all went back to living in the White House kennel—and Ford never suggested taking care of them again.

"Tell me, General, how dead is the Dead Sea?"
—Vice President George Bush to Jordanian chief of
staff Zeid Bin Shaker

Cashing Out

When Grover Cleveland was drafted into the Union Army during the Civil War, he did what any other red-blooded American would do—he paid a substitute $150 to take his place. What Cleveland did was completely legal under the terms of the Conscription Act of 1863. Yep, you could pay some poor sap a couple hundred dollars and he would go fight in your place. Cleveland decided he should stay at home and support his mother and sister while his two brothers were off fighting for the Union. His actions were made a part of his opponent's campaign during Cleveland's presidential race; but since it was legal, it had no impact on the voters. Cleveland didn't dodge the draft—he met it head on with a handful of money.

"I don't think you're going to see a great, great uproar in this country about the Republican committee trying to bug the Democratic headquarters." —President Richard Nixon, a short four days after the Watergate break-in

A Red Letter Day

In 1950, Harry S Truman's daughter, Margaret, gave a singing recital in Washington. Her performance was attacked in a review by the *Washington Post* music critic, Paul Hume. When President Truman read the review he was incensed. Truman wrote the following letter to Hume: "I have just read your lousy review buried in the back pages. You sound like a frustrated old man who never made a success, an eight-ulcer man on a four-ulcer job, and all four ulcers working. I have never met you, but if I do you'll need a new nose and plenty of beefsteak and perhaps a supporter below."

Hume published the note hoping to embarrass the president. But it did just the opposite—most Americans approved of Truman's stance. Years later Margaret Truman wrote, "Dad never felt the slightest remorse about sending it. He always insisted that he had a right to be two persons—the president of the United States and Harry S Truman, father of Margaret, husband of Bess Wallace. 'It was Harry S Truman, the human being, who wrote that note,' he said."

No wonder his nickname was "Give 'Em Hell" Harry.

At the time President Abraham Lincoln was assassinated the only money he had on his person was a five-dollar Confederate note.

Wrong Place at the Wrong Time—Three Times Running

Robert Todd Lincoln, Abraham Lincoln's eldest son, is the only person to have been at the scene of three presidential assassinations. On April 14, 1865, the day his father was shot, Robert Todd rushed to Ford's theater to be with his fatally injured father. In 1881 he was in the same room with President Garfield the day he was assassinated. And twenty years later, he was to join President McKinley at the Pan American Exhibit when McKinley was assassinated—arriving shortly after the assassination. There are many mysterious and bizarre happenstances about Abraham Lincoln's life and death and so too with Robert Todd. You see, the son of the president would never have witnessed any of these assassinations had he not narrowly escaped death at a young age. While standing on a crowded railroad platform, he stumbled and nearly fell onto the tracks. He was grabbed by the back of the shirt and pulled to safety in the nick of time. The person who saved his life was Edwin Booth—the brother of John Wilkes Booth.

"I can still remember the first time I ever heard Hubert Humphrey speak. He was in the second hour of a five-minute talk." —Gerald Ford on vice presidential and, later, presidential hopeful Hubert Humphrey

State of the Union

While President Ronald Reagan's plane was circling over Forbes Field near Topeka, Kansas, waiting for clearance to land, security officers noticed a potential hazard. Two dogs were mating on the runway. These same two dogs had resisted earlier attempts to uncouple and were now "taxiing down the runway." The officers claimed the two copulating canines posed a danger to Reagan's plane and therefore did the only thing they could think of—they shot them. I don't think the dogs were looking to threaten *Air Force One*—they just wanted to fly United.

The only two politicians bound by law never to travel together are the President and the Vice President.

What's in a Name?

Ulysses Simpson Grant was born in 1822, to Jesse and Hanna Grant. Actually, I'm lying. Jesse and Hanna Grant did have a baby boy, but they didn't give him a name for a full month. When they finally did name him he was called Hiram Ulysses Grant: Hiram for his grandfather, and Ulysses for the Greek hero. When Hiram joined the U.S. Military Academy, he was incorrectly listed by his congressman as Ulysses Simpson Grant. Grant, who always disliked his name because of what his initials spelled, H.U.G., decided to keep his newly appointed name. He never adopted the name formally but used it as his own for the rest of his life. It was probably a good thing that he used Ulysses—I can't imagine people voting for a Hiram, can you?

"A politician is a man who approaches every problem with an open mouth." —Democratic presidential nominee Adlai Stevenson

Fostering Ill Will

In 1989, John Hinckley, Jr., the man who shot President Ronald Reagan in order to impress actress Jodie Foster, went to court seeking permission to communicate with the press. Hinckley wanted to persuade the press to be more unbiased in its reporting of him and to stop its "image of me as this sick, depressed psychotic person." A psychiatrist argued that Hinckley was still not well and to prove his claim presented letters that Hinckley had written during the previous two years. In one letter, Hinckley referred to Charles Manson as a "prophet" and in another he asked his correspondent, "Why not draw a picture of Jodie Foster for me in the nude?" At least he's not so crazy as to refer to Jodie Foster as a prophet and ask for a nude drawing of Charles Manson.

"I've read about foreign policy and studied—I know the number of continents." —1968 presidential hopeful George Wallace

Return to Sender— Address Unknown

Lincoln's Gettysburg Address is considered one of the most moving and brilliantly written speeches of all times. And the most fascinating aspect of the speech is that Lincoln wrote it on the back of an envelope on the train to Pennsylvania. Wrong! It would be wonderful to believe this masterpiece was so divinely inspired that Lincoln dashed it off in a matter of minutes. But the truth is, Lincoln began working on the Gettysburg Address eleven days before he gave the speech on November 19, 1863. In fact there are five drafts of the speech still in existence—some even written on White House stationery. It is possible that what people saw on the train was Lincoln putting the final touches to the speech—or jotting down his grocery list.

In 1978, President Jimmy Carter, the first Southerner elected to the presidency following the Civil War, restored U.S. citizenship to Jefferson Davis, president of the Confederate States of America.

Bucking the System

"The Buck Stops Here," the phrase popularized by Harry S Truman, which meant he was ultimately responsible for the actions of his administration, had nothing to do with money. The buck President Truman was referring to was a knife with a buckhorn handle. During a card game, in order to keep track of whose deal it was, the buckhorned knife, or "buck," was placed in front of the player with the deck. Hey, learn something new every day.

Samuel Mudd, the doctor who treated the broken ankle of Lincoln's assassin, John Wilkes Booth, received a presidential pardon in 1869 from Ulysses S. Grant.

The Saga of the First President

Here's something about the presidents we all know is correct—George Washington was the first president of the United States. Nope. Think about this: The original thirteen colonies of the United States claimed their independence from England through the Declaration of Independence signed in 1776. Okay. Now, George Washington wasn't elected president of the United States until 1789. That means there was a gap of thirteen years between the founding of our nation and the election of the first president. Then who ran the country during those first thirteen years? John Hanson, that's who. John Hanson was elected "President of the United States in Congress Assembled" by a unanimous vote of Congress on November 5, 1781.

He served for one year.

Hanson was then followed by Elias Boudinot, the second president of the United States. And Thomas Mifflin, the third president. Richard Henry Lee, the fourth. Nathan Gorman, the fifth. Arthur St. Claire, the sixth. Cyrus Griffin, the seventh. And good old George Washington, the eighth.

**Because George Bush was a chubby toddler, his father
referred to the future president as "Fatty McGee McGaw."**

The Saga of the First President—Volume II

Okay, now we know George Washington was actually the eighth president of the United States. So why were we taught he was the first? The reason is that George Washington was the first president to rule the United States under the Constitution, which was ratified in September 1787. The seven people before Washington, Hanson being the first, served as president under the Articles of Confederation, which only brought the thirteen colonies together in a "league of friendship" called the Continental Congress.

There was no provision in the Articles of Confederation for a central government—all government at that time was on the local level. So it wasn't until the passage of the Constitution and then the Bill of Rights that a federal government was created. That's why scholars don't believe that John Hanson was really the first president of the United States. But what have other people said about it?

"Mr. President. I feel very sensibly the favorable declaration of Congress expressed by your Excellency." —George Washington to John Hanson, shortly after Hanson was elected president

"[George] Washington accepts every condition, law, rule and authority, under the Great Seal and the first President of the United States, John Hanson." —Thomas Jefferson, secretary of state to George Washington

Was John Hanson the first president of the United States? You can believe who you want—a tweed-coat-wearing scholarly type or Thomas Jefferson and George Washington themselves.

As a joke, Andrew Jackson sent out formal invitations to the annual Christmas ball to a mother-and-daughter team well known as prostitutes in Salisbury, North Carolina. No one thought it was particularly funny.

The Saga of the First President—Volume III

We know a lot about George Washington, whom we thought was the first president of the United States; but what do we know about the real first president, John Hanson? He took office on November 5, 1781, just about the time the Revolutionary War ended. One of his first acts as president was to order all foreign troops off U.S. territory. Once all the foreign troops were gone, there wasn't a need for such a large standing army in the United States—so Hanson had the militias reduced. Not an easy task, owing to the fact that the United States didn't have enough money to pay the existing soldiers for their tour of duty. Soon, the unpaid soldiers were marching on Washington and threatening to take over the new government by force. What did the members of the Continental Congress do? They left town—all of them—except John Hanson. He stood up to the mutineers and negotiated a peaceful settlement with them. That in itself should rank as a highlight of his short one-year term, but he also created the Department of Foreign Affairs, the Treasury Department, and the position of secretary of war. There's more: He chartered a national bank and created a postal service. He is even credited with creating the national holiday that we still celebrate on the fourth Thursday of every November—Thanksgiving. Here's a question for those who still doubt John Hanson was the first president of the United States—if he wasn't, where did he get the authority to do all these things?

"There's nothing left but to get drunk." —President Franklin Pierce in 1856—after having his renomination for the presidency rejected by his own party—responding to the question "What will you do after leaving office?"

Where's My Script?

"The problem is—the deficit is—or should I say—wait a minute, the spending, or gross national product, forgive me—the spending is roughly 23 to 24 percent. So that it is in—it's what is increasing, while the revenues are staying proportionately the same and what would be the proper amount they should, that we should be taking from the private sector." —President Ronald Reagan, answering reporter's questions off the cuff

George Washington didn't have enough money to get to his own inauguration and was forced to borrow six hundred dollars from a neighbor.

Still Here in Spirit

President Clinton has been criticized for having a large number of "friends" spend the night in the Lincoln bedroom. But there's one guest who keeps showing up uninvited—Lincoln himself. There have been a number of reports of "Lincoln sightings" by such distinguished people as Winston Churchill and Theodore Roosevelt. During her visit to the White House, Queen Wilhelmina of the Netherlands told others she had answered a knock at her door, only to find Lincoln standing there. The queen promptly fainted. Of course, hearing a knock on any door inside the White House and opening it to find Bill Clinton standing there wouldn't be such a shock anymore.

Theodore Roosevelt sued the editor of *Iron Age* magazine for calling him a drunk and won— Roosevelt was awarded six cents.

A Party that
Would Raise the Dead

A contest was announced in 1998 that offered couples the opportunity to enjoy fine wine and a seven-course meal in the company of a United States president. The only drawback was that the president had been dead since 1881. Cleveland's Lake View Cemetery sponsored an essay contest in which the first prize was a tour of the cemetery and then a gourmet meal of Beluga caviar, Gulf shrimp, homemade sorbet, and champagne at the monument of slain American president James A. Garfield. The essay: You had to explain why you wanted to win. Retirees Ernest and Sally Horvath won the contest and celebrated their forty-ninth anniversary in the Cleveland cemetery. Ernest's essay told of how he proposed to Sally while the two were visiting the picturesque graveyard some fifty years ago. The two winners were joined by actors who portrayed the president and Mrs. Garfield. "Even though the Garfield Monument has been around for 108 years, most people in Cleveland don't know it exists," said William Garrison, president of Lake View Cemetery Association. I hate to burst your bubble, Mr. Garrison, but few people remember that James A. Garfield was president.

"The thought of being president frightens me and I do not think I want the job." —Ronald Reagan, 1973

A Timely Death

In 1992, according to the White House office of presidential inquiries, President George Bush once received a letter inviting him to attend a funeral. There's nothing very odd about this—a president gets this type of request all the time. The letter described the man whose funeral Bush was invited to attend as "hard-working" and "patriotic." The letter went on to explain that the man in question wasn't dead yet but was on life support—and the plug could be pulled at any time in order to accommodate the president's schedule.

"There they are—See No Evil, Hear No Evil, and Evil."
—Bob Dole commenting on the gathering of former
presidents Gerald Ford, Jimmy Carter, and Richard Nixon

Hot Off the Presses

A year after Woodrow Wilson's first wife, Ellen Louise Axson, died in the White House, the president was seen with the widow Edith Galt at the theater. The *Washington Post* reported that instead of watching the show, "the President spent most of his time entering Mrs. Galt."

It was, of course, a typographical error. The sentence was supposed to read "entertaining" Mrs. Galt. Or did the press know something we didn't?

"I think the American public wants a solemn ass as president. And I think I'll go along with them."
—Calvin Coolidge

Grant the Vegan

Although Ulysses S. Grant was known as a hard-drinking man's man and a fierce soldier, he became squeamish at the sight of animal blood. He rarely ate meat and when he did, it had to be cooked overdone. He couldn't even stand the thought of eating poultry. "I could never eat anything," he confessed, "that went on two legs." For breakfast, he usually ate a cucumber pickled in vinegar. The rest of the day he was usually pickled himself.

"Well, there doesn't seem to be anything else for an ex-president to do but go into the country and raise big pumpkins." —Chester A. Arthur

Who Am I Now?

"First I was Millie's co-owner. Then it was Barbara's husband, the author of the best-selling book. And now it's the father of the governor-elect of Texas. And then I have to share Dana Carvey. Not going to do it. Wouldn't be prudent. Not going to do it." —George Bush, during the groundbreaking ceremonies of the George Bush Presidential Library at Texas A&M University in 1994

No president has been an only child.

It's Not Who You Know—It's Who You're Related To

The monarchs of past—kings, queens, princesses, princes, dukes, and earls—were all related to each other. It made for some bad blood but great family reunions. In American history we know that some presidents were related—the Harrisons, the Roosevelts, the Adamses—but it goes a little further than that. In fact, the family tree of American presidents has more forks than a formal dinner setting. Here's what I mean:

Richard Nixon was a distant cousin of both William H. Taft and Herbert Hoover.

Zachary Taylor was Confederate President Jefferson Davis's father-in-law.

Theodore Roosevelt was Franklin D. Roosevelt's fifth cousin.

Martin Van Buren was Theodore Roosevelt's third cousin twice removed.

Ulysses S. Grant was Grover Cleveland's sixth cousin once removed.

John Adams was John Quincy Adams's father.

John Tyler was Harry S Truman's great-uncle.

Zachary Taylor was Robert E. Lee's fourth cousin once removed.

Benjamin Harrison was William Henry Harrison's grandson.

"The most terrifying words in the English language are, I'm from the government and I'm here to help."
—Ronald Reagan

The Poltergeist Express

It is rumored that the ghost of Abraham Lincoln walks the halls of the White House, but what does he do when he's tired of walking? He takes the train. Beginning on April 27, 1866, the year after President Lincoln was assassinated, and for several years thereafter, on an area of railroad track near Albany, New York, the phantom of Lincoln's funeral train has been spotted. April 27 coincides with the date Lincoln's body was carried on that particular stretch of track.

In 1995, officials in Belfast debated over whom they should invite to light the city's Christmas tree: President Clinton or the Mighty Morphin Power Rangers.

Socks's Dad Socks Back

Usually the president deals with the press with kid gloves—but when conservative newspaper columnist William Safire called Hillary Clinton a "liar," President Clinton wanted to deal with him with boxing gloves. The President threatened the newspaperman with a "forceful response to the bridge of Mr. Safire's nose." Safire responded by thanking the President for providing him with "historic notoriety." He stated that with the blizzard that was blanketing the East at the time, "hardly anybody in Washington received that issue of the paper."

"I will not accept if nominated and will not serve if elected. . . . If forced to choose between the penitentiary and the White House for four years . . . I would say the penitentiary, thank you." —Civil War General William Tecumseh Sherman when asked to run for the presidency in 1884

Too Close for Comfort

When he was two years old, Herbert Hoover nearly died of the croup. His parents couldn't hear his breathing or feel his heart beating. They gave him up for dead, placing pennies on his eyelids and covering his face with a sheet. Fortunately, Hoover's uncle, Dr. John Minthorn, arrived in time to revive him. It's a lucky thing for the American people that Hoover lived—we needed a scapegoat for the Great Depression.

"I was never popular. . . . Without my glasses I was blind as a bat, and to tell the truth, I was kind of a sissy."
—Harry S Truman on his childhood

Read My Lips

President George Bush made the expression "Read My Lips" part of the national vernacular during his presidential campaign in 1988. He made the promise of no new taxes. And sure enough, as soon as he was elected president he raised taxes. He didn't call them taxes, however; they were referred to as "receipts proposals" and "user fees," but they still tallied up to $21.7 billion in his 1991 budget. We did read his lips—we just didn't know which face he was using at the time.

James Garfield had a dog named Veto.

A Timely Idea

It's a well-known fact that clocks on display are set at 8:20 to honor the time of Abraham Lincoln's death. Sorry again—not true. Abraham Lincoln is known to have died at 7:30—not 8:20. So why are clocks set at 8:20? Well, they're really not set at 8:20 either—they're actually set at 8:18 for the simple reason that it looks nice . . . it's symmetrical and aesthetically pleasing to the eye. The other reason is because the manufacturer's name can be seen better if the hands of the clock aren't in the way. The Lincoln thing is a nice thought though.

When King George VI and Queen Elizabeth visited the White House in 1939, Eleanor Roosevelt served them hot dogs for dinner.

First Day on the Job

Presidents weren't born presidents; they had to have some other job before they landed the big one. At age ten, Bill Clinton's first job prepared him for his future in politics. Clinton's grandfather Eldridge Cassidy hired young Bill to stand in front of his general store in Hope, Arkansas, and greet each and every new customer with a cheerful hello and a hardy handshake. Clinton fondly recalled his first job: "I liked telling people 'Hello,' and at quitting time I got paid in all-day suckers." There's a joke there somewhere but I'll let you fill in the blank.

"It's a very good question, very direct, and I'm not going to answer it." —President George Bush in 1990 when asked what type of deficit-reduction proposals he would present to Congress

The Move that Crowned Dick a King

The infamous "Checkers Speech" given by vice-presidential candidate Richard Milhous Nixon saved his career. Nixon had been accused of having an $18,000 slush fund that he used to pay off expenses. It would have been enough to ruin his political career—if he were a mere mortal politician and not "Tricky Dick." Nixon spent $75,000 of Republican National Committee money and bought thirty minutes of national television time. In that thirty minutes Nixon saved his political skin. He told the viewing public that he and his wife had a small savings account and drove a two-year-old Oldsmobile. He did admit to accepting a gift, however:

> A man down in Texas heard Pat on the radio mention the fact that our two youngsters would like to have a dog and, believe it or not, the day before we left on this campaign we got a message from Union Station in Washington that they had a package for us. We went down to get it. You know what it was? It was a little cocker spaniel in a crate that had been sent all the way from Texas—black and white, spotted, and our little girl Tricia, the six-year-old, named it Checkers. And you know, the kids, like all kids, loved the dog, and I just want to say this right now, that regardless of what they say about it, we are going to keep it.

Nixon never mentioned the slush fund but his crafty and political game of "Checkers" saved his vice-presidential nomination—which he won on the Eisenhower ticket. Checkers went to the big kennel in the sky in 1964 and is buried at the Bide-A-Wee Pet Cemetery on Long Island. There is discussion by the Nixon Library to have Checkers exhumed and reburied next to the president in Yorba Linda, California. I think after all this time we should just let sleeping dogs lie—I'm talking about Checkers, of course.

At his first inauguration (administered by Robert R. Livingston of New York), George Washington added the "so help me God" to the end of the oath of office.

Love at First Sight

Grace Goodhue was an attractive single woman who was also a well-liked teacher at an institute for the deaf. One day, while watering the school's garden, she heard someone whistling. She looked up and saw, through the window of a nearby boardinghouse, a man standing in front of a mirror wearing only a pair of longjohns with a hat perched on his head. Ms. Goodhue thought it was a funny sight and let out a laugh. "He heard me and turned to look at me," she recalled later. "When he learned who I was, he managed to arrange a formal introduction—and that is how I became Mrs. Calvin Coolidge."

"My God, this is a hell of a job! I can take care of my enemies all right. But my damn friends, my God-damn friends. . . . They're the ones that keep me walking the floor nights!" —Warren G. Harding on the presidency

Movin' On Up!

It has long been rumored that Thomas Jefferson, the third president of the United States, had a long-standing relationship with one of his slaves, Sally Hemings. Sally was not only his slave but she was also the half sister of Jefferson's wife, Martha. Not only did they have a relationship—but it was rumored that he fathered five children with her. Well, that's not true—he only had one with her. According to a study reported in the November 1998 issue of the science journal *Nature,* DNA tests show "almost total, complete similarities" between Jefferson's DNA and the DNA of Eston Hemings. "I have found that we have strong genetic evidence, but not absolute proof, that Eston Hemings, who was Sally Hemings's last child, was probably fathered by Thomas Jefferson," said retired Tufts University School of Medicine pathology professor Dr. Eugene Foster, who headed the study.

Dr. Foster also conducted DNA matching on Thomas Woodson, the first son of Sally Hemings, but the tests showed that Jefferson was not his father. "We found that Thomas Woodson, who was the ancestor of a large African-American family who believed that Thomas Jefferson was their father, we have found no evidence to support that," Foster said. However, John Taylor King, a Woodson descendant and retired president of Huston-Tillotson College in Austin, Texas, stands by the oral histories that have been passed down from generation to generation. "We contend [Jefferson] was not a philanderer. He was 33 when his wife died, and he fell in love with Martha's [his wife's] half sister [Sally Hemings] and they were together for 36 years. That's part of our family history and we stand by it," he said.

Foster and his team also disproved another rumor that Jefferson's nephews, Samuel and Peter Carr, were actually the fathers of Sally Hemings's children—

which would have explained the physical similarity between Jefferson and Hemings's children. "We examined the descendants of Samuel and Peter Carr and find no evidence they had anything to do with the paternity of the child of Sally Hemings," Foster said.

It is not only contradictory that the man who coined the phrase "All men are created equal" should own slaves but Jefferson himself must have known something was going on—the only slaves he ever freed were the children of Sally Hemings.

During the 1984 Presidential campaign, Democratic candidate Walter Mondale said, "George Bush doesn't have the manhood to apologize." To which George Bush responded "Well, on the manhood thing, I'll put mine up against his any time."

I Don't Think So!!!

"We in America today are nearer to the final triumph over poverty than ever before in the history of any land. The poorhouse is vanishing from among us. We have not yet reached the goal but, given a chance to go forward with the policies of the last eight years, we shall soon with the help of God be in sight of the day when poverty will be banished from this nation." —Herbert Hoover in 1928, accepting the Republican nomination for president. Less than a year later the country fell into the depths of the Great Depression after the stock market crashed.

Most military experts agree that George Washington was a good general but not a great one. His army lost more battles than it won.

The Comeback Trail

It was a hot day in the nation's capital on the Fourth of July 1850, and President Zachary Taylor was out celebrating with the crowd. While attending the festivities in front of the Washington Monument, the president suffered sunstroke and decided to retire to the White House. In order to cool down Taylor partook of a cool, refreshing snack. He gobbled down a huge bowl of cherries and washed them all down with a pitcher of iced buttermilk. Surprisingly enough, he became violently ill and was dead four days later. The official diagnosis was gastrointestinal infection, but there was also a rumor that the sixty-five-year-old president may have been murdered. A little more than 130 years later, while doing research on her book about Taylor, historical novelist Clara Rising heard the murder theory again and again. She convinced Taylor's descendants and the courts to allow Taylor's body to be exhumed and examined for possible arsenic poisoning. Bill Maples, a prominent forensic scientist from Florida, who once examined the bones of John Merrick, aka "The Elephant Man," was chosen to do the pathology report. Taylor's body was exhumed in 1991 and Maples collected hair, nail, and bone samples from the former general and twelfth president of the United States. After careful examination Maples came to the unmistakable conclusion that Taylor hadn't been murdered by arsenic poisoning or any other type of poisoning. He died of gastrointestinal infection, Maples observed, because the buttermilk was probably spoiled.

Andrew Jackson's pet parrot, Poll, was ejected from the room during Jackson's funeral in June 1845 because he kept squawking obscenities at the mourners.

By Any Means Necessary

Here's another well-known fact about Lincoln: The Emancipation Proclamation freed the slaves, right? Well . . . no. We are taught, in the shorthand version of American history, that the Emancipation Proclamation freed the slaves. But actually, the Proclamation, issued by President Abraham Lincoln on January 1, 1863, proposed freeing the slaves in the Southern states only. But since those states had seceded, Lincoln had no authority over them. He was just using his Proclamation to scare the South into rejoining the Union. Lincoln's real reason for the Proclamation was made very clear in a letter to the *New York Times*: "My paramount objective in this struggle is to save the Union, and is not to save or destroy slavery. If I could save the Union without freeing any slaves I would do it, and if I could save it by freeing all slaves I would do it; and if I could save it by freeing some and leaving others alone I would do that."

Although we are all taught that Lincoln's Emancipation Proclamation freed the slaves—it didn't. What did free the slaves was the Thirteenth Amendment to the Constitution, which was ratified in the latter part of 1865—and unfortunately, Lincoln was dead by that time.

"Voters quickly forget what a man says."
—Richard M. Nixon

Any Last Words?

Presidents are quoted all the time. Sometimes they say funny things—sometimes they say wise things. Sometimes they say stupid things. So what's the last thing on a president's mind before he dies? Read on:

"Good morning, Robert." —The last words of Calvin Coolidge

"I am about to die. I expect the summons very soon. I have tried to discharge my duties faithfully. I regret nothing, but I am sorry that I am about to leave my friends." —Zachary Taylor's last words

"I am going," said John Tyler to his attending physician.
"I hope not, sir," replied the doctor.
"Perhaps it is best," John Tyler added. These were his last words.

In 1848, after suffering a stroke in the Capitol building, John Quincy Adams died. His last words were: "This is the end of Earth; I am content."

"Nothing more than a change of mind." —James Madison's last words

George Washington, who had a fear of being buried alive, made an order his last words:
"I am just going," he said. "Have me decently buried and do not let my body be into a vault in less than two days after I am dead. Do you understand me?"
"Yes," replied his aide.
" 'Tis well." These were the last words of George Washington.

On April 12, 1945, just when Franklin D. Roosevelt was about to see World War II brought to an end on both the European and Pacific fronts, and while an artist was sketching his portrait, he suddenly pressed his hand to his forehead and cried out, "I have a terrific headache."

During his youth, Bill Clinton, along with two other boys, performed in a jazz combo called the Three Blind Mice. They all wore sunglasses.

"The Eyes Seem to Follow Me"

In the annual group photograph of the Iowa senate's pages there is one person missing—President Clinton. The traditional photograph is always taken in front of the senate president's chair, which includes the official White House portrait of the sitting President. But in the 1998 photograph, the senate pages, made up of high school students, voted to remove the portrait of President Bill Clinton. "He's not the best role model for young people," said Matt Johnston, a senate page from Muscatine, Iowa. Others mimicked Johnston's remark citing Clinton's, at that time alleged, affair with White House intern Monica Lewinsky. With all the scandals that have surrounded the President, it's hard to tell if he was framed, nailed to a wall, or captured on linen.

"Blessed are the young, for they shall inherit the national debt." —President Herbert Hoover

What's Up, Doc?

President Jimmy Carter loved to fish in secluded lakes. It was the only place on earth where he could be alone. So when Carter went fishing on a small lake near his home in Plains, Georgia, he didn't expect any company—certainly not a crazed, rabid river rabbit. Here's the scene: Carter was on the lake in a canoe when he saw a wild-eyed, furry woodland creature leap into the lake hissing and baring its teeth. The attack rabbit headed straight toward him. In describing the event, Carter said, "I had the paddle in the boat, so when the rabbit got closer for me to recognize it, and I saw it was going to attempt to climb in the boat with me, I thought that would be an unpleasant situation for me and the rabbit." Carter took the paddle and slapped the water in front of the rabbit to discourage it from "climbing aboard." From here, the reports are unclear as to what became of "killer rabbit" or "Bonzi bunny," as the animal was tagged by the press. Senator Bob Dole, who was running in the 1980 presidential election against Carter, explained, "I'm sure the rabbit intended the President no harm. In fact, the poor thing was simply doing something a little unusual these days—trying to get aboard the President's boat. Everyone else seems to be jumping ship."

Near the end of his presidency, we all knew Jimmy Carter was up a creek—we just didn't know he had a paddle.

"I have left orders to be awakened at any time in case of national emergency, even if I'm in a cabinet meeting."
—Joke by Ronald Reagan in retaliation to the press attacks that he slept during crises

Auction Blockade

When President Lincoln died there was no "Presidential Widow's Fund" to help take care of his wife, Mary Todd Lincoln. Embarrassed by her situation but in desperate need of money, Mary Todd, using the pseudonym Mrs. Clarke, contacted a New York broker, W. H. Brady. She told Brady she wanted to sell some of her jewelry, fine clothes, and other personal belongings. When other brokers discovered the identity of "Mrs. Clarke," they accused her of stealing the items from the White House. Suddenly, no one was interested in purchasing Mrs. Lincoln's possessions. Brady quickly returned the now-priceless artifacts to Mrs. Lincoln—along with a bill for $800. Eventually, however, a pair of earrings and a brooch did sell at auction—for a lot more than expected. The items were assessed at around $1,800 but surprisingly they sold for $18,400. Unfortunately, Mary Todd didn't see a penny of this money because the auction was held on October 20—1998!

"It has been said by some cynic, maybe it was a former president, 'If you want a friend in Washington, get a dog.' Well, we took them literally—that advice, as you know. But I didn't need that because I have Barbara Bush." —President George Bush

V.P., D.O.A.

Gerald Ford's presidency is one of the few that wasn't awash in controversy. He was dubbed "Mr. Nice Guy" and most people liked him—although he was harassed for his occasional slips and falls. Too bad the same couldn't be said about his vice president, Nelson Rockefeller. A call to police brought the paramedics to the apartment of one of Rockefeller's aides, twenty-five-year-old Megan Marshak. The woman told police the seventy-year-old vice president was there "editing an art book." What the police found was a table set with food and wine, Rockefeller lying dead on the floor sans shoes and socks, and Ms. Marshak dressed in a long black evening gown. The police also never recovered any art or any manuscript.

President Clinton got into trouble with that woman, Monica Lewinsky—but at least his intern didn't cause him to be interred.

**While former president Dwight D. Eisenhower was
visiting Walter Reed Army Hospital in May 1965,
someone stole the spare tire from the trunk of
his 1964 Lincoln Continental.**

King for a Day

People have always made fun of the vice president. And many a presidential race has been lost because voters didn't like the choice of VP. But that's not the case of Franklin Pierce. In fact, Franklin Pierce won the presidency even though his vice president didn't do a single day of campaigning. Why didn't his VP campaign? Because William Rufus De Vane King, Pierce's running mate, was holed up in Havana, Cuba, dying of tuberculosis. They made a great team, however. Pierce was such a known heavy drinker that Republicans referred to him as "a hero . . . of many a well-fought bottle."

Pierce was able to get his drinking under control well enough to make it through four years in the White House—unfortunately, King didn't fare as well. He was so sick that he was unable to make it back to Washington for his inauguration. Instead, a special act of Congress allowed King to take his oath of office in Cuba—making him the only executive officer of the United States to have been sworn in on foreign soil. That is the only impact King had on American politics; he died six weeks after taking office and never spent a single day of his vice presidency in Washington.

"When more and more people are thrown out of work,
unemployment results." —Calvin Coolidge

Finally, an Honest
Politician

Here is an exchange that took place in 1956 between then Senate majority leader Lyndon Baines Johnson and *Newsweek* reporter Sam Shaffer.

"If you want to know what Lyndon Baines Johnson was going to do at the national convention," Johnson yelled, "why didn't you come to Lyndon Baines Johnson and ask him what Lyndon Baines Johnson was going to do?"

"All right," said Shaffer, trying not to buckle, "what is Lyndon Baines Johnson going to do at the convention?"

"I don't know" was Lyndon Baines Johnson's response.

**Among other things, Thomas Jefferson was an architect.
He designed and built a unique structure on the
White House grounds, complete with classical
columns—a hen house.**

Let's Make a Deal

Here's how it went: Spiro Agnew resigned after allegations over bribe-taking had surfaced. Richard Nixon appointed Gerald Ford to take Agnew's place as vice president. When Richard Nixon resigned after Watergate, Gerald Ford took over as president of the United States, and he appointed Nelson Rockefeller as his vice president. Shortly after taking the reins of power, Gerald Ford granted Richard Nixon a full pardon for any crimes he may have committed in regard to Watergate. Then Ford lobbied Congress to award former President Nixon $850,000 to cover his expenses while Nixon made the transition from the White House to civilian life.

Ford considered the sum of $850,000 a compromise deal owing to the fact that the Presidential Transition Act of 1963 provides ex-presidents (who complete their full term in office) one million dollars to cover their expenses during this six-month transition period. Yep, presidents get one million dollars after they leave office to help them settle into the world they helped create. Congress came up with a deal of their own; they decided to give Nixon only $200,000 to help him make the transition. So basically, for destroying the trust of the American people, Nixon still got a library named after him and a couple hundred thousand dollars, courtesy of the taxpayers. Nice deal, wasn't it?

While serving as governor of Georgia, and prior to becoming president, Jimmy Carter appeared on *What's My Line* and nearly stumped the panel.

The Heart of the Matter

"I try not to commit a deliberate sin. I recognize that I'm going to do it anyhow because I'm human and I'm tempted. And Christ set some almost impossible standards for us. Christ said, 'I'll tell you that anyone who looks on a woman
with lust in his heart has already committed adultery.' I've looked on a lot of
women with lust. I've committed adultery in my heart many times." —President
Jimmy Carter in an interview with *Playboy* magazine in 1976

"A little rebellion now and then is a good thing."
—Thomas Jefferson

Lincoln's Emancipation

The Clintons made having a cat in the White House fashionable—but animals have found haven in the executive mansion for many years. One of the most interesting pets came into the Lincoln White House as a gift for Thanksgiving: Abe's admirers sent him a huge turkey. Lincoln's son, Thomas (Tad), who was about ten years old at the time, named the bird Jack and made him his pet. Tad was devastated when he found out Jack was going to be the guest of honor at Thanksgiving—as the main course. He threw a fit and appealed to his father to give the turkey a reprieve, at least until Christmas. President Lincoln agreed and granted a stay of execution for Jack.

When Christmas time rolled around, Tad again pleaded with his father for mercy. At one time he made such a commotion his father had to temporarily adjourn a cabinet meeting to see what all the screaming was about. When Honest Abe realized Tad was begging for the life of his pet, he walked back into his office, picked up a pen and piece of paper, and wrote out a document releasing Jack from his impending demise. Tad, waving the document around and screaming for joy, ran into the kitchen and showed the cook he would have to come up with another idea for Christmas dinner.

"Nobody likes to be called a liar. But to be called a liar by Bill Clinton is really a unique experience." —Ross Perot, presidential candidate, 1992 and 1996

Sounded Like a
Good Reason at the Time

On July 2, 1881, while waiting for a train at the B&O station in Washington, D.C., President James Garfield was shot by an anarchist named Charles Guiteau. Guiteau shot Garfield in the lower back and also grazed his right arm with a five-barrel, .44-caliber pistol called a British Bulldog. Guiteau claimed he used this unique collector's item because he thought it would look great on display in a museum after the assassination. And he was probably right—except for one thing: more than a hundred years after he took the life of President Garfield, no one knows where the gun is located.

The Smithsonian doesn't know. The National Archives doesn't know. The FBI doesn't know. Even the U.S. Attorney's office, which prosecuted the case, doesn't know. So the gun never made it on display—but what is on display from this tragic event in American history is: Guiteau's skeleton (but not his skull), a portion of Guiteau's brain (the other portion was used for medical study), and, don't ask me why, Guiteau's spleen. All can be found (if you're really interested) at the National Museum of Health and Medicine at Walter Reed Army Medical Center in Washington, D.C. The museum also has three of President Garfield's vertebrae, which were struck by Guiteau's bullet. But, as fate would have it, the main reason for Garfield's assassination is nowhere to be found.

**President Bill Clinton's favorite relish is
watermelon rind pickle.**

Henpecked President

Calvin Coolidge wasn't just known for being quiet; he was also known for being a tightwad. During his presidency, "Skin-flint" Coolidge tried to raise chickens at the White House. But every time one of his yard-raised chickens was served for dinner it tasted strange. Finally, the mystery of the foul-tasting fowl was solved when someone explained to Coolidge that his chickens were penned over the same spot where Theodore Roosevelt had once grown mint. Now, if one of the former presidents had just grown rosemary or sage, Coolidge would have been eating preseasoned chicken.

President Andrew Jackson once received a gift of a 1,400-pound wheel of cheese from a New York dairy farmer. The president invited the public on a "first come, first serve" basis to help themselves.

Presidential Firsts

George Washington was the first and only president elected by a unanimous electoral vote.

Richard Nixon was the only person ever elected twice to both the office of president and the office of vice president. He also holds the distinguished honor of being the only president ever to resign.

Abraham Lincoln was the first and only president to receive a patent. Patent #6469 was a very complex device, much like car safety air bags of today, that used chambers of air to help heavy ships pass through shallow water.

Andrew Jackson was the first president to be handed a baby to kiss during his campaign. He refused to kiss the infant and instead handed the baby over to his secretary of war.

Herbert Hoover was the only president who turned his entire salary over to charity.

Woodrow Wilson was the only president to have earned a Ph.D. He earned it from Johns Hopkins University in 1886.

"Of course, I may go into a strange bedroom every now and then that I don't want you to write about, but otherwise you can write everything." —Known womanizer Lyndon B. Johnson in a statement to the press

The Laugh-In Was on Us

What was the turning point in the 1968 presidential race that changed people's point of view of Richard Nixon? Believe it or not, it was his brief appearance on the television show *Laugh-In*. When Richard Nixon, the staunch, tight-suited, sweaty, humorless politician, stood in front of the camera and said "Sock it to me" on the hippest show on television, people started thinking differently about him. It was a close race, but in the end Nixon slid by Democrat Hubert Humphrey to win the election. Humphrey himself was asked to appear on the same episode of *Laugh-In* as Nixon—he was supposed to say "Sock it to him, not me" right after Nixon's appearance—but Humphrey declined. After Nixon's appearance, Humphrey sensed the change in attitude toward Nixon and asked to appear on the show himself—but it was too late. The American voters did "sock it to" Richard Nixon—and during Watergate he socked us right back!

**James Buchanan was the only bachelor president
ever to occupy the White House.**

Grant Needed a Grant

After Ulysses S. Grant left office he was persuaded to invest his life savings in a banking firm that was partnered by one of his sons. Grant handed over $100,000, which was nearly everything he had, expecting his money would grow at an impressive rate. But it turned out that the head of the company was a con artist who embezzled from the company, forcing it into bankruptcy in 1884. Now the eighteenth president of the United States was broke. And he was also diagnosed with terminal throat cancer (Grant smoked twenty cigars a day). He had no way of earning money and wanted desperately to leave something behind for his wife. Enter circus impresario P. T. Barnum. Barnum offered Grant $100,000 if he would go on a nationwide tour along with his personal memorabilia—sort of a traveling ex-president's show. Grant thought about it, but the hero of the Civil War couldn't see himself placed on display for a bunch of gawking onlookers. Grant refused the money. Instead, Grant, in a race against death, began writing his memoirs. He continued writing them until the day he died. Mark Twain published Grant's autobiography after the president's death—and the royalties from the sale of the book earned Grant's widow more than $500,000. Barnum coined the phrase "There's a sucker born every minute," but in this case Ulysses S. Grant wasn't one of them.

As a young law student at Duke University Law School, Richard Nixon was reprimanded after being caught breaking into the dean's office.

In Space No One Can Hear You Scream

We've all heard stories about President Bill Clinton's alleged sexual escapades. The President is an earthy guy, but according to Long Beach, California, UFO expert Dr. Terry Johnson, for the last fifteen years Bill has been having an affair that's out of this world. In February 1998, Dr. Johnson claimed that for the last fifteen years Bill and Hillary Clinton have been routinely abducted by aliens and forced to have sex. The aliens' purpose? To create half-human, half-alien embryos to be raised by the extraterrestrials. Dr. Johnson also warns that if anyone attempts to ask the President or First Lady about their "space sex" they won't get an answer—the aliens have erased the Clintons' memories of the abductions. Maybe the aliens erased Clinton's memory of all his sexual liaisons—that would explain a lot.

"If you've seen one redwood tree, you've seen them all."
—President Ronald Reagan

A Pair of Affairs

Earlier in this book I mentioned that Warren Harding loved dogs—but he loved something else, too: women. Harding was known to have had at least two affairs while he was married: one with Carrie Phillips, the wife of Harding's good friend Jim Phillips; the other with Nan Britton, a woman he met while editing his newspaper, the *Marion Star.* The fact of the affair with Carrie Phillips was taken care of early so as not to affect Harding's chance of becoming president. She was offered $25,000 and $2,000 a month if she would take a long vacation—for as long as Harding was in office. She did—and the affair wasn't discovered until after Harding died. The Nan Britton affair also didn't surface in the papers until after Harding died—but everyone in the White House knew about it, including Harding's wife. Harding and Nan were known to sneak off and consummate their affections for each other in a White House closet. Then Nan got pregnant and soon had a little girl named Elizabeth Ann who looked remarkably like Harding. Harding kept his word to Nan and continued to support her and the baby financially; he also promised to marry her when his wife died and be a good father to his daughter. But Harding died before his wife and Nan got nothing. She had kept their relationship under the covers for too long and decided she could make a little money by revealing their relationship between the covers of a book. She wrote *The President's Daughter,* which became a bestseller and was eventually made into a movie, in 1928, called *Children of No Importance.* The rumor that Harding's death was actually a well-disguised murder by his wife is starting to make more and more sense, isn't it?

"You don't set a fox to watching the chickens just because he has a lot of experience in the hen house."
—Harry Truman on Richard Nixon's candidacy, 1960

A Slave to Fashion

A lot of revisionists (people who want to rewrite history to make it politically correct) have torn into President Thomas Jefferson because he owned slaves. Some have even gone so far as to suggest removing his picture from the $2 bill (yes, there is a $2 bill). But if you're going to do that we're going to be short a lot of money. Nine other presidents have also owned slaves: Washington (on the quarter and the $1 bill), Andrew Jackson ($20 bill), and Ulysses S. Grant ($50 bill). The other presidents are James Madison, James Monroe, John Tyler, James Knox Polk, Zachary Taylor, and Andrew Johnson—they owned slaves but aren't on U.S. currency.

If Jefferson is elected, "murder, robbery, rape, adultery, and incest will be openly taught and practiced."
—John Adams's campaign propaganda against opponent Thomas Jefferson

Hero Today—
Gone Tomorrow

"Man Saves President Ford's Life by Deflecting Assassin's Gun" was the headline that splashed across newspapers on September 22, 1975. While President Gerald R. Ford was visiting San Francisco, a woman, Sara Jane Moore, broke from the crowd, pulled out a gun, and aimed it at the president. Fortunately, a bystander, Oliver Sipple, lunged at the woman and threw her to the ground just as the gun went off. The bullet missed hitting President Ford by only a few feet. Sipple, an ex-marine, was an instant hero. The press hounded him for interviews and photographs but Sipple just wanted to be left alone. Reporters began digging into Sipple's private life and soon uncovered the fact that he was gay—something Sipple hadn't told his family. The national hero pleaded with the press to keep his private life out of the papers—but when the media gets ahold of a story like that, it's like asking a starving dog to give up a meaty bone. So the next day, the *Los Angeles Times* ran a front-page story headlined "Hero in Ford Shooting Active Among S.F. Gays." I guess even the press couldn't bring themselves to print "Queen Saves President." When Oliver Sipple's mother found out about her son—not that he saved the president's life but that he was gay—she stopped speaking to him. And when she died in 1979, Sipple's father refused to allow him to attend her funeral. His own life, after saving the life of the president, became so hopeless that Sipple began drinking heavily. He was found dead in his apartment of "natural causes" in 1979—he was only thirty-seven years old. There's nothing the press likes more than to take a bite out of a hero.

"I am a man of limited talents from a small town. I don't seem to grasp that I am President." —Warren G. Harding

You Spell Potato and I Spell Potatoe

When Vice President Dan Quayle was visiting a Trenton, New Jersey, elementary school in June 1992, he thought it would be a good photo op to take over the emceeing of the spelling bee. When it was sixth-grader William Figueroa's turn, Quayle asked him to spell the word "potato." Figueroa did—and did it correctly. But the vice president insisted the twelve-year-old put an "e" at the end of it. "I knew he was wrong," Figueroa later told reporters, "but since he's the vice president, I went and put the 'e' on and he said, 'That's right, now go and sit down.' Afterward, I went to a dictionary and there was *potato* like I spelled it. I showed the reporters the book and they were all laughing about what a fool he was." Figueroa became an overnight celebrity and the vice president became an overnight idiot. Little William Figueroa later appeared on *Late Night with David Letterman* and even led the pledge of allegiance at the 1992 Democratic National Convention. He was later hired as a spokesperson for a company that makes a computer spelling program. Dan Quayle went on to pick a fight with a fictional television character—Murphy Brown.

"If it were not for the reporters, I would tell you the truth." —Chester A. Arthur

More Presidents on the Presidency

Here are more insights into what the most powerful man on earth has to say about his job.

"I am in jail, and I can't get out. I've got to stay."
—Warren G. Harding on his life as president

"My movement to the chair of Government will be accompanied by feelings not unlike those of a culprit who is going to the place of his execution." —George Washington on the presidency

"This job is nothing but a twenty-ring circus—with a whole lot of bad actors." —Herbert Hoover

"It sure is hell to be president." —President Harry "Give 'Em Hell, Harry" Truman, during his first year as president

"This planet is our home. If we destroy the planet, we've destroyed our home, so it is fundamentally important."
—"Master of the obvious" and Independent
presidential candidate, H. Ross Perot

Autograph Hound

In the early 1960s columnist Leonard Lyons taunted President John F. Kennedy with remarks that Kennedy's signature was only worth $65 to collectors. Lyons tried to embarrass the president with the comparison between the value of his signature and the going price of other presidents' signatures—George Washington's was valued at $175 and Franklin Roosevelt's at $75. Kennedy, knowing the ribbing was in good fun, responded in writing to the newspaperman, and at the bottom of the letter wrote: "Dear Leonard: In order not to depress the market any further, I will not sign this letter."

And he didn't.

Franklin D. Roosevelt vetoed a record-setting 635 bills during his four terms as president.

High-Sounding Speaker

When one thinks about President Abraham Lincoln, the image of a tall, bearded, deep-voiced man comes to mind. Well, he was tall and bearded but he didn't have a deep voice. In fact, Lincoln's voice was high-pitched, shrill, and piercing. Not a very good attribute for today's politicians, but during the days of open-air speeches and debates, Lincoln's voice could be clearly heard hundreds of yards away while his opponents' faded off.

Gerald Ford was sworn in as president a short twenty-eight minutes after the Secretary of State received Richard Nixon's letter of resignation.

A One-Man Party

President William Howard Taft was used to throwing his weight around—all 300+ pounds of it. One story goes that Taft was stranded at a train station in the country and there were no regular train stops scheduled that evening. There was, however, an express train that passed by the station, but it would stop only for "large parties." Taft sent a wire to the conductor at a station en route informing him to "Stop at Hicksville. Large party waiting to catch train." When the conductor pulled the train into the station, he looked around and only saw the rotund figure of William Howard Taft, who, without missing a beat, informed the conductor, "You can go ahead. I am the large party."

Ronald Reagan, "The Great Communicator," is the only president to have performed in Las Vegas.

The President
and the King

Not everyone liked President Richard Nixon, but the king did. I'm not talking about the king of some foreign land, I'm talking about "The King"—Elvis Presley. Elvis thought J. Edgar Hoover was "the greatest living American ... [and Richard Nixon] ... wasn't far behind." On December 21, 1970, Elvis dropped by the White House unannounced, requesting an audience with the president. To make sure Nixon knew who he was, he brought along a letter to introduce himself. It seemed Elvis was interested in becoming a federal agent to help fight the drug problem—the country's, not his. In his letter he wrote that "The drug culture, the hippie elements, the SDS, Black Panthers, etc." did not consider him as part of the establishment and therefore he would be able to easily infiltrate their ranks. To help Nixon realize that he knew what he was talking about, Elvis wrote that he had done an "in-depth study of drug abuse" as well as "Communist brainwashing techniques."

Nixon did see Elvis, who was stoned on painkillers during the meeting. Needless to say, his request to be made a federal agent was denied.

Abraham Lincoln is the only U.S. president who was also a licensed bartender. Lincoln was co-owner of Berry and Lincoln, a saloon in Springfield, Illinois, and he needed a license to sell alcohol.

It Was Twenty
Years Ago Today

Another popular "weirdness" is the "twenty-year curse." Beginning in 1840 and continuing for more than one hundred years, every president elected in a year ending in a zero died in office.

- **William Henry Harrison, elected in 1840**
  Harrison gave the longest inaugural address in history. He didn't wear a coat, hat, or gloves. He caught a cold and died of pneumonia a month later.
- **Abraham Lincoln, elected in 1860 and reelected four years later**
  On April 14, 1865, Lincoln was assassinated.
- **James A. Garfield, elected in 1880**
  Garfield was shot on July 1, 1881, and died three months later.
- **William McKinley, elected in 1900**
  McKinley was shot in the back on September 6, 1901, and died eight days later.
- **Warren G. Harding, elected in 1920**
  Harding died of an apparent heart attack after two and a half years in office. (There are questions about the actual cause of his death. Some theorize that Mrs. Harding may have done away with her two-timing husband.)
- **Franklin D. Roosevelt, elected in 1940 for a third term**
  Roosevelt died of a cerebral hemorrhage on April 12, 1945, less than four months after taking the oath of office for a fourth term.

- **John F. Kennedy, elected in 1960**
  Kennedy was assassinated on November 22, 1963.
- **Ronald Reagan, elected in 1980**
  Reagan broke the chain of the "twenty-year curse" but not by much. Reagan was shot and wounded by John F. Hinckley approximately two months after taking office. Quick medical treatment is credited with breaking the curse.

I'm not putting a jinx on anyone, mind you, but it will be interesting to see who gets elected in the year 2000—and what happens.

"Well, David, did you do any fornicating this weekend?"
—Richard Nixon's question to David Frost
shortly before an interview

All Washed Up

The Secret Service agent is sworn to protect the president at any and all costs—even to give up his or her life if necessary. So when President Clinton decided to take a swim at Daytona Beach, Florida, three Secret Service agents assigned to protect him had no choice but to follow him into the ocean. When they trudged out of the water, not only were they wet—they had been soaked: Their badges, wallets, jewelry, sunglasses, watches, hotel room keys, and other personal belongings, including their socks and shoes, had all been stolen.

**"Some reporters said I don't have any vision.
I don't see that." —President George Bush**

Presidential Hopefuls

Usually, during a presidential race, we only hear about the two main people running against each other from the two major parties—unless, of course, Ross Perot is running. But there are a number of people who register with the U.S. Federal Election Commission to have their names placed on the ballot. In 1992, for instance, there were a record 273 registrants. On the commission's 1996 alphabetical list immediately preceding Bill Clinton's name is Billy Joe "Won't Pull Your Leg" Clegg. Billy Joe was supported by his Biloxi, Mississippi, "Just Kaus" presidential campaign committee. So instead of getting a Billy who won't pull your leg, we got one who will.

Franklin D. Roosevelt served a record 4,422 days as president of the United States.

Ladies in Waiting

Franklin D. Roosevelt was confined to a wheelchair because of the polio that paralyzed his legs—but he wasn't a "man of steel" because of the chair. FDR also went head-over-wheels for the ladies. His first mistress was Lucy Mercer, Eleanor Roosevelt's social secretary. When Eleanor found out about the affair, she told FDR she would let him out of their marriage. Roosevelt refused the offer because (A) Lucy was Catholic and wouldn't marry a divorced man and (B) FDR knew his mother would cut him out of the inheritance. So he broke off the affair and went in search of someone else. He found her in the pool—the secretarial pool, that is. And she had the perfect name for a mistress—Missy LeHand. FDR and Missy's relationship was no secret to anyone—she lived in her own set of rooms at the White House and could regularly be seen seated upon the president's lap or in his personal suite. Fate intervened on their relationship when Missy suffered a cerebral hemorrhage and eventually died. This left the president on the outs, and before he had to dip back into the pool, his old flame Lucy Mercer reentered the picture. Lucy's husband had also suffered a stroke, leaving her a free woman. But the third stroke wasn't one of luck for FDR—it was his own, a massive cerebral hemorrhage that took his life in Warm Springs, Georgia. Roosevelt's mistress Lucy Page Mercer was with him at the time and was quickly hustled away before Eleanor arrived. Makes the whole Bill Clinton/Monica Lewinsky thing seem a little tame, doesn't it?

James Garfield was the first president to use a phone in the White House. His first words to inventor Alexander Graham Bell, who was on the other end, were "Please speak a little more slowly."

A Long-Awaited Payoff

President Ulysses S. Grant respected the noted philanthropist Horace Norton and presented him with a cigar in 1862. Norton saved the cigar as a memento and treated it reverently. He even passed the cigar on to his son. His son, in turn, passed it on to his son, Winstead Norton. In 1932, some seventy years later, Winstead delivered a speech at a reunion, and as a tribute to both his grandfather and Ulysses S. Grant, lit the cigar in their memory. The crowd grew hushed as Winstead put the flame to the tip of the cigar—then suddenly, BANG! The cigar exploded. Ulysses S. Grant had given Horace Norton a trick cigar and it took seventy years for Grant to finally get his little joke. It's probably just as well—I don't think a seventy-year-old cigar would have tasted too good anyway.

"This is a great day for France!" —President Richard Nixon while attending Charles de Gaulle's funeral

More Presidential Firsts

During his time, it was fashionable for men to wear breeches (short pants), but Thomas Jefferson was the first president who insisted on wearing long pants.

Gerald Ford became the thirty-eighth president after Nixon resigned: Ford then nominated Nelson Rockefeller as vice president. They became the nation's first unelected presidential team.

John Tyler was the first president to marry while in office.

Franklin D. Roosevelt was the first president elected to a third term (in 1940). He was also the only president ever elected to a fourth term, in 1944. There will never be another president eligible for a third or fourth term in office; in 1951, the Twenty-Second Amendment to the Constitution was adopted, limiting presidential service to two terms.

During George Washington's first year as president he operated a ferry service that ran back and forth across the Potomac River.

Curiouser and Curiouser

There have been numerous similarities drawn between Abraham Lincoln and John F. Kennedy, probably stemming from their most striking similarity—they were both assassinated. Here are the facts:

- Lincoln began a term in Congress in 1847; Kennedy was elected to Congress exactly one hundred years later.
- Lincoln was elected president in 1860, Kennedy in 1960.
- Both Lincoln and Kennedy are known for advancements in civil rights.
- Both were shot on a Friday.
- Both were in the presence of their wives.
- Both were shot from behind and in the head.
- Lincoln and Kennedy were succeeded in death by southern Democrats named Johnson (Lincoln: Andrew Johnson; Kennedy: Lyndon B. Johnson)
- The slain presidents' successors had both held seats in the U.S. Senate.
- Andrew Johnson was born in 1808, Lyndon Johnson in 1908.
- Both presidential assassins were known by their full names: John Wilkes Booth and Lee Harvey Oswald.
- John Wilkes Booth was born in 1839. Lee Harvey Oswald was born in 1939.
- Booth and Oswald were southerners who championed unpopular ideas: Booth was a secessionist; Oswald was a pro-Castro communist.
- Both presidents had children die while in the White House.

- President Lincoln's secretary, whose name was Kennedy, advised him not to go to the theater.
- Kennedy's secretary, whose name was Lincoln, advised him not to make the trip to Dallas.
- Both presidents had premonitions about their assassinations. Hours before his death, Lincoln said to White House guard William Crook, "If it is to be done, it is impossible to prevent it." Kennedy said, "If somebody wants to shoot me from a window with a rifle, nobody can stop it, so why worry about it?"
- John Wilkes Booth shot Lincoln in a theater and hid in a warehouse.
- Lee Harvey Oswald shot Kennedy from a warehouse and hid in a theater.
- The names Lincoln and Kennedy each contain seven letters.
- The car Kennedy was riding in when he was assassinated was a Lincoln.
- The names Andrew Johnson and Lyndon Johnson each contain 13 letters.
- Both Johnsons were opposed for reelection by men whose names start with "G."
- Both assassins were killed before they could be brought to trial.

These similarities are frightening—if you're a conspiracy-theory paranoid. The author has uncovered two more similarities.

- Two years before he was assassinated, Abraham Lincoln was visiting Monroe, Maryland; two years before Kennedy was assassinated, he was visiting Marilyn Monroe.
- In 1996 Oakland Raiders tackle Lincoln Kennedy, on his decision not to vote, said, "I was going to write myself in, but I was afraid I'd get shot."

Weird. Creepy. Bizarre. Or just the rambling imagination of someone with too much time on their hands? You be the judge.

When President Warren G. Harding was short of funds during his twice-a-week poker games, he routinely used pieces of fine White House china to raise the ante.

Also Rans

A number of people have run for president throughout the years. For example, Dr. Benjamin Spock, noted physician and baby-book author, ran for president in 1972 on the People's Party ticket. The thought of having a president who knows how to handle babies makes a lot of sense to me: The president has to deal with Congress, remember? Another presidential contender was Wavy Gravy (aka Hugh Romney), who nominated a pig for president in 1968 and has sponsored the Nobody for President campaign in every election since 1972. Abbie Hoffman, cofounder of the Yippies, and his merry band gathered outside the Democratic National Convention in Chicago in 1968 and also nominated a pig ("Pigasus") for president. Unfortunately, we'll be without Pat Paulson in the presidential elections of the future—Paulson, of *Laugh-In* fame, is a candidate who will be missed.

While a captain, Ulysses S. Grant was asked to resign from the army because he was drunk so often.

In the Nick of Time

Growing up, most of us had nicknames, I suspect. The presidents had them, too—not just when they were growing up but when they were in the White House, as well. Some were nice—others weren't. Here's a sample:

Because of his girth, Grover Cleveland was called "Uncle Jumbo."

Owing to the fact that he wore glasses and had a Ph.D., Woodrow Wilson was nicknamed "Professor."

Legend has it that Calvin Coolidge rarely spoke more than a few words at a time and was therefore called "Silent Cal." (The truth is, Calvin Coolidge gave more press interviews than any president up to that time.)

Gerald R. Ford's nonaggressive, easy-to-get-along-with nature earned him the title "Mr. Nice Guy."

Richard Nixon was called "Gloomy Gus" in college, and because he spent so much time studying he was also called "Iron Butt." When he ran for Congress in 1950, he earned the title "Tricky Dick."

Warren G. Harding probably had the saddest nickname; he was called "Everybody's Second Choice."

"I'm surprised that a government organization could do it that quickly." —President Jimmy Carter in 1979, while visiting Egypt, after hearing the Great Pyramid at Giza took twenty years to build

Better than a
Box of Chocolates

Seventeen women in Turda, Romania, lined up in front of a stand-up photograph of President Bill Clinton. They were competing in a Valentine's Day contest to see who could best imitate Clinton's first meeting with former White House intern Monica Lewinsky. The lucky winner was eighteen-year-old Diana Ciurtin. In her reenactment of that ill-fated encounter, Ciurtin dropped to her knees and offered the photograph-clad figurine a cup of coffee. "Mr. President, I hear we have a common passion, the saxophone," she said. "Would you let me play your saxophone?" Ciurtin's first-place prize was a free dinner at a local restaurant and free professional hairstyling for a year.

**"My father used to say that it was wicked to go fishing
on Sunday. But he never said anything about
draw-poker." —President Grover Cleveland**

Political Twain Stop

There's been a great deal of talk about character issues and presidents recently. So it makes sense that in the "good old days" character issues weren't a problem. Right? Well, here is an article by Mark Twain, who decided to run for president in 1896, discussing his character issues.

I have pretty much made up my mind to run for President. . . . I am going to own up in advance to all the wickedness I have done, and if any Congressional committee is disposed to prowl around my biography in the hope of discovering any dark and deadly deed that I have secreted, why— let it prowl.

I candidly acknowledge that I ran away at the Battle of Gettysburg. . . . I want my country saved, but I preferred to have somebody else save it. I entertain that preference yet. . . . The rumor that I buried a dead aunt under my grapevine was correct. The vine needed fertilizing, my aunt had to be buried, and I dedicated her to this high purpose. Does that unfit Me for the Presidency? The Constitution of our country does not say so. . . . I admit also that I am not a friend of the poor man. I regard the poor man, in his present condition, as so much raw material. Cut up and properly canned, he might be made useful to fatten the natives of the cannibal islands and to improve our export trade with that region.

It's probably a good thing Mark Twain didn't run for the position seriously—if he had won, he may have been the third president assassinated. Why? Because the candidate who did win the 1897 presidential election was William McKinley!

"I've noticed that nothing I never said has hurt me."
—President Calvin "Silent Cal" Coolidge

Baiting the President

The *Deh Cho Drum* newspaper from Fort Simpson in the Northwest Territories of Canada isn't the most well-known paper in the world. It has a small circulation of about 1,200, which serves a handful of isolated aboriginal communities. But the editor, Arthur Milnes, went on a fishing expedition trying to lure a big fish to do a guest column—and landed him. Milnes knew former U.S. President George Bush had been fishing in the North so he sent Bush a letter to see if the president would write a column about his thoughts on fishing for arctic char.

A few weeks after he sent the letter, in September 1997, Milnes arrived at his one-man office to discover that Bush had submitted the requested guest column.

"I couldn't believe it when I saw it on the fax machine," said Milnes. "Then I nearly fell off my chair when I phoned the number on the fax to thank the president for taking the time and they put me right through to him."

During their conversation Bush, like most novice writers, was concerned about how his column would be received by fishing fanatics.

"He said he didn't want them to think he was trying to sound like an expert or anything," Milnes said. "I assured him that he didn't sound that way—anything but—and that I thought the people of the North would be as thrilled as I was that he had been so moved by our area of Canada that he had taken the time to write for such a small publication."

Now we know the answer to that age-old question—what do former presidents do with all their free time?

A survey conducted by New Jersey–based Leflein Associates in March 1998 reported that 94 percent of American women say they've never fantasized about President Bill Clinton.

The Wrong Address

Even though Lincoln's Gettysburg Address, given on November 19, 1863, is considered one of the most eloquent orations in American history (quite a feat seeing that the entire speech is only 271 words long), the *Chicago Times* hated it. The day after Lincoln's speech, which dedicated the battlefield cemetery, the *Times* wrote: "The cheek of every American must tingle with shame as he reads the silly, flat and dish-watery utterances of the man who has been pointed out to intelligent foreigners as the President of the United States."

It was so bitterly cold at Ulysses S. Grant's presidential inauguration that the canaries that were supposed to sing at the inaugural ball froze to death.

One Man, One Vote—
And That's All

He was called "Old Rough and Ready," but Zachary Taylor was never ready to enter the world of politics. In fact the first political race he ever voted in was the presidential race of 1848—in which he was a candidate. Taylor attributed his absentee voting to the fact that he was too busy fighting wars in defense of our country: specifically the War of 1812 and Texas's war for independence from Mexico. When one of Taylor's aides first mentioned the possibility of the general running for the presidency, Taylor was reputed to have said "Stop your nonsense and drink your whiskey!"

Taylor was nominated by the Whig Party, but he didn't find out about the nomination until weeks after the convention. He was sent a formal letter of notification but refused to accept it—there was ten cents in postage due. He never read the letter and had it returned unopened. The committee soon sent him another letter, prepaid this time. Taylor opened it, learned he had been chosen as the Whig's presidential nominee, and headed off to Washington.

**"The second office of the government is honorable
and easy, the first is but a splendid misery."
—Thomas Jefferson, in 1797, on the vice presidency
and the presidency, respectively**

Were Warren's Words Wasted?

"Progression is not proclamation nor palaver. It is not pretense nor play on prejudice. It is not of personal pronouns, nor perennial pronouncement. It is not the perturbation of a people passion-wrought, nor a promise proposed." Makes one passionately ponder what Harding's partly persuasive but preposterous pronouncement meant.

James Madison was the smallest president ever. He measured five feet four inches and never weighed more than one hundred pounds.

Two Prints of
Three Stooges

During an auction in New York City in 1993, a photograph autographed by former Presidents Gerald Ford, Jimmy Carter, and Richard Nixon sold for $275. A photograph signed by the Three Stooges, Larry, Moe, and Curly, went for $1,870.

In an effort to watch his waistline, President Richard M. Nixon often dined on cottage cheese and ketchup.

A Real Shot in the Arm

Will the Kennedy assassination coincidences ever end??!! In December 1993, James Leavelle (he's the man in the white hat handcuffed to Lee Harvey Oswald when Oswald was shot by Jack Ruby) was giving an interview to a reporter. Retired Dallas police officer Leavelle was re-creating for newsman Bob Porter how he grabbed Ruby's gun to prevent him from shooting Oswald again. With the cameras rolling, and using the same model gun Ruby had used, Leavelle accidentally shot Porter in the arm. Porter was rushed to Parkland Hospital—the same hospital both Kennedy and Oswald were sent to. But, unlike the other two, Porter survived.

"It is about a socialist, antifamily political movement that encourages women to leave their husbands, kill their children, practice witchcraft, destroy capitalism, and become lesbians." —Televangelist Pat Robertson, 1988 GOP presidential candidate, speaking out on the proposed Equal Rights Amendment in Iowa in 1992

One Cool President

On July 1, 1881, President James Garfield was in the waiting room at the Baltimore and Potomac railroad station with his two sons, Harry and James. Suddenly, thirty-nine-year-old Charles J. Guiteau rushed the president, pulled out a .44 British Bulldog revolver, and fired two shots. The president dropped to the floor. It took a full seventy-five minutes for an ambulance to arrive and take the wounded president back to the White House. The doctors believed the president's liver had been damaged and gave him only a few hours to live. But a few days later with his temperature hovering just below 100 degrees and his breathing greatly improved, it looked like Garfield was on his way to a full recovery. Then Washington's notorious July heat struck. "If it would even cool off a little at night as it always did in my father's log cabin," he told his wife, Lucretia, "I believe I would begin to improve." Chatting about their childhood (they grew up in the same town), they recalled the olden days when they used to saw huge chunks of ice from the pond and store it for warmer weather. Then Lucretia had an idea. "Ice!" she cried. "That's it! Ice!" Mrs. Garfield left the stricken president and yelled out instructions to her aides. "Go out and buy every pound of ice you can find! Hurry! This stifling air is killing the president!" Soon the president's bedroom was filled with buckets, pails, and tubs of ice, and his family took turns waving palmetto fans to circulate the cooler air. The president smiled gratefully and rested. An inventor, who had heard about the ill president, devised a method whereby cheesecloth soaked in ice water was blown upon with a fan. This did make the room cooler—but it was so humid the president could barely breathe. Then the director for the Geological Survey, John Wesley Powell, improved upon the idea by using huge blocks of ice to cut down on the moisture and a series of ducts to carry away the melting ice. On July 12, 1881, the world's first "air conditioning machine" was put into action—and it was a success. Unfortunately things weren't looking too good for the president. He died after serving only 199 days in office, 79 of which were spent in unbearable pain from his gunshot wounds.

So as not to be understood by guests, Herbert Hoover and his wife sometimes spoke Chinese to each other.

Me and My Shadow

Corruption in high places usually makes the news—but does anyone remember what happened to Vice President Spiro T. Agnew? His resignation was overshadowed by a little thing called Watergate. But let's revisit Mr. Agnew's moments of glory, shall we? Agnew had quickly climbed the political ladder starting as Baltimore county executive, then on to governor of Maryland. Nixon discovered Agnew, liked his strong "law and order" stand, and asked him to be his vice-presidential running mate. Agnew was elected VP on Nixon's ticket in 1968, and then again in 1972. It was thought that Agnew had been accepting bribes since his early days in politics, and the possibility existed that he was even accepting them as vice president. At first Agnew called the allegations "damned lies." But when a federal grand jury began hearing the case, he quickly pleaded no contest to the charge of evading income tax on the pay off money. The most damning evidence came when Agnew told the court that in Maryland, political bribes are so commonplace that businesses simply budgeted for them. Seeing the end of his political career, Agnew resigned as vice president in October 1973—during the throes of the Watergate scandal. Nixon resigned the presidency in August 1974, and if Agnew hadn't been caught before that, he would have become the thirty-eighth president of the United States.

In 1995, during the Bob Hope Golf Classic, Bill Clinton scored 100, Gerald Ford hit a spectator with a ball, and George Bush struck two—one of the wounded onlookers required ten stitches on her nose.

You Don't Say

"You can fool all the people some of the time and some of the people all of the time, but you can't fool all of the people all of the time" is a quote made famous by President Abraham Lincoln, right? Sorry. This remark is not found in any of the writings of Abraham Lincoln nor can it be found in any newspapers in Lincoln's time. In fact, the saying did not surface until more than fifty years after Lincoln was supposed to have said it. Most historians now attribute the remark to circus impresario P. T. Barnum. But nearly 150 years later it seems this old saying isn't quite true—seems that all of the people were fooled for all this time.

"The United States is at peace with all the world, and sustains friendly relations with the rest of mankind."
—President Benjamin Harrison, spoken while addressing Congress

He Got More than Fries
with That Burger

Having your name associated with President Clinton isn't always a good thing—just ask Charlie Shaw. In February 1994, Clinton passed by Shaw's deli in London, Ohio, and noticed a sign advertising "Clinton Burgers." The President couldn't resist eating something named after him, so he popped into the deli to grab a bite to eat. Shaw served the President the specially prepared "Clinton Burger"—a beef patty with bacon, cheese, mushrooms, and onions, all topped with a secret "Clinton Sauce." Soon the Clinton Burger was making the news and Shaw was getting a lot of attention. Unfortunately he caught the attention of a Madison County health inspector, too. It turned out that Shaw didn't have a food-service permit—so the President gobbled down a burger at a place that wasn't legally allowed to sell food. Not only that, but it turns out that the summer before Shaw had pleaded guilty to state Agriculture Department charges that he was selling meat illegally—and that his deli had unsanitary conditions. He was fined $200 and court costs. If that's not enough to turn your stomach, just the thought of eating anything smothered in something called "Clinton Sauce" makes me a little squeamish.

"Well, I don't have much job security." —Bill Clinton in 1992, when asked why he continues to play the saxophone

Shin Guards

In 1958, while serving as vice president under Dwight D. Eisenhower, Richard Nixon made a visit to Venezuela. A protester broke from the crowd, ran up to Nixon, and spit on him. The protester was quickly apprehended by Secret Service men who held him at the vice president's request. Nixon then approached the protester, looked him in the eyes, and kicked him in the shin. Nixon admitted in his book *Six Crises* that "nothing I did all day made me feel any better." The more one learns about Richard Nixon the more endearing he becomes.

The body of John Scott Harrison, father of President Benjamin Harrison, was stolen by grave robbers and sold to Ohio Medical College in Cincinnati for use as a training cadaver. The body was recovered and reinterred.

Presidents on Presidents

Everyone has an opinion of any number of former presidents. But what have presidents and former presidents said about their peers? You might be surprised.

"His brain could have been compressed within the periphery of a nutshell." —Andrew Johnson's assessment of President Ulysses S. Grant

"The General doesn't know any more about politics than a pig knows about Sunday." —Harry S Truman's take on President Dwight David Eisenhower (1952)

"Damn the president! He is a cold-blooded, narrow-minded, prejudiced, obstinate, timid old psalm-singing Indianapolis politician."
—Theodore Roosevelt's opinion of President Benjamin Harrison (1890)

"He's like a Spanish horse who runs faster than anyone for the first nine lengths and then turns around and runs backward. You'll see, he'll do something wrong in the end. He always does." —A prophetic Lyndon Baines Johnson on Richard Nixon

"He was another one that was a complete fizzle. . . . Pierce didn't know what was going on, and even if he had, he wouldn't have known what to do about it." —Harry S Truman's opinion of President Franklin Pierce

"He is too illiterate, unread, unlearned for his station and reputation." —John Adams on George Washington

Gerald Ford's name before he was adopted was Leslie Lynch King, Jr. And Gary Hart's real name is Gary Hartpence.

A Little Bit Off the Top

It was called the "haircut heard around the world." In May 1993, President Clinton received a $200 haircut on *Air Force One* by well-known hairstylist Christopher. An expensive haircut, to be sure, but that wasn't the problem. At the time, *Air Force One* was parked on the tarmac at the Los Angeles Airport (LAX). The press printed the information that according to a Federal Aviation Administration official, the haircut closed down air traffic on LAX's four runways for nearly an hour. So much bad publicity was generated that the hairstylist, Christopher, held a press conference—which, in and of itself, is a unique thing in American politics. Christopher adamantly denied that the President was a self-important, stylish, stuck-up man. "I am not saying this in a negative way," he told reporters, "but from what you can see, do you really think that Hillary or Bill Clinton are very concerned about their appearance?"

After the hoopla over the event cooled down, it was uncovered that the whole thing may have been the work of political opponents. When someone actually went to the trouble of checking the airport's records, it was discovered that no runways were shut down and no planes were kept waiting.

Frank Johns, presidential candidate on the Socialist Labor ticket in 1928, was a true hero. He drowned in a river while trying to rescue a young boy.

Other than That, How Did You Like the Play, Mrs. Lincoln?

Ford's Theater, the site of Lincoln's assassination, is now a popular working theater and Lincoln museum. But following the assassination in 1865, an angry mob gathered in front of the theater and wanted to burn it to the ground. Police dispersed the crowd and the theater was saved. The federal government decided to buy the theater from the owner, John Ford, for the sum of $100,000. As with most things associated with Lincoln, the theater, which was turned into an office building, had its own troubles. In 1893 the building collapsed, killing twenty office workers and injuring sixty-eight others. After the horrible accident the building was abandoned and began to deteriorate. A group of concerned Americans petitioned the government to save the historic landmark. In 1964, restoration on the building was complete and Ford's Theater once again looked as it did in 1865. And here's another fun little twist: Who was the first president to visit Ford's Theater after its reconstruction? John F. Kennedy? No, that would have been a perfect ending to the Lincoln/Kennedy connection, but sadly, Kennedy was dead before the building was complete. The first president to visit Ford's Theater after the reconstruction was—Gerald R. Ford.

"Why do you come and ask me, the leader of the
Western world, a chicken-shit question like that?"
—President Lyndon B. Johnson's response to
a reporter whose question he found trivial

Does the Alma Matter?

Nowadays we wouldn't think of electing a president who hadn't gone to college. One would hope that all the presidents had learned in the hallowed halls of a university—not so. There were nine presidents who never attended college:

George Washington
Martin Van Buren
Millard Fillmore
Andrew Johnson
Harry Truman

Andrew Jackson
Zachary Taylor
Abraham Lincoln
Grover Cleveland

When you look at the fact that Abraham Lincoln didn't attend college and someone like Warren Harding did, it makes you wonder if a degree is all it's cracked up to be.

President George Bush banned broccoli from the menu of *Air Force One*.

Presidential Singsong

Nearly every presidential campaign had a song or a slogan: "I Like Ike," "All the Way with LBJ," and the like. Most of the time the songs were written to promote the candidate; other times the songs were written to tear the opponent down. During the campaign between Martin Van Buren and William Henry Harrison (which many consider the first modern-day presidential campaign), songs, slogans, and the "Born in a Log Cabin" story were all used. Harrison, known for his victory at the battle of Tippecanoe, was nicknamed "Tippecanoe"; hence his slogan, "Tippecanoe and Tyler, Too," Tyler being John Tyler, his vice-presidential running mate. Here is a stanza from the campaign song of Harrison's opponent, Martin Van Buren.

Sung to "Rock-a-Bye Baby"

Hush-a-bye baby, Daddy's a Whig
Before he comes home hard cider he'll swig
Then he'll be tipsy and over he'll fall
Down will come Daddy, Tip, Tyler, and all.

Yep, dirty politics has been around for a long time.

"Never trust a man unless you've got his pecker in your pocket." —Lyndon B. Johnson

The Assassination Nation

We all know Presidents Abraham Lincoln and John F. Kennedy were assassinated; the two other assassinated presidents that some have a problem remembering are William McKinley and James Garfield. But there were several presidents whose lives were threatened by an assassin. Here is a synopsis of the "Greatest Hits of the Presidents."

President Andrew Jackson. January 30, 1835, in Washington D.C. Richard Lawrence approached the president with two loaded pistols—both of which misfired. The president was unharmed.

Theodore Roosevelt, former president and then presidential candidate on the Bull Moose ticket. October 14, 1912, in Milwaukee. Shot by John Schrank. The bullet passed through Roosevelt's folded script, kept in his breast pocket. Roosevelt continued his speech and was then taken to the hospital where he made a full recovery.

Franklin Roosevelt (president-elect). February 15, 1933, in Miami. Shot at by Joseph Zangara, an anarchist. The bullet missed the president and killed the mayor of Chicago, Anton Cermak, instead.

President Harry Truman. November 1, 1950, in Washington, D.C. The president was staying at Blair House while the White House was under repair; Griselio Torresela and Oscar Collazo, both Puerto Rican nationalists, attempted to storm the building and assassinate the president. Blair House guard Leslie Coffelt and Torresela were killed during the confrontation. Truman was unharmed.

To be continued . . .

"Follow me around. I'm serious. If anybody wants to put a tail on me go ahead. They'd be very bored." —Presidential candidate Gary Hart, in 1987, shortly before the Donna Rice scandal caused him to drop out of the race

The Genie Is Out of Service

"My little man, I am making a strange wish for you—it is that you may never be president of the United States." Statement made by President Grover Cleveland to a five-year-old Franklin D. Roosevelt, who was visiting the White House. Cleveland's words fell on deaf ears and Roosevelt went on to be elected a record four times as president.

Ronald Reagan was the first president ever to be divorced.

The Eagle Has Landed

When Dolores Delgadillo of Dallas, Texas, saw President Clinton riding a train to the Democratic National Convention in August 1996, she had an idea. Ms. Delgadillo was upset that Amtrak was proposing to close the Texas Eagle train service and thought Vice President Al Gore might be an ally.

"The train has been our mainstay for visiting family in Chicago, and now that we're grandparents, for visiting grandchildren on both coasts," Delgadillo wrote. "Yet your administration is killing the Texas Eagle."

Gore's staff's written response, and apparently their train of thought, was a little off track: "I share your view that the urgent problem of species extinction and the conservation of biological diversity should be addressed. All plants and animals help make our natural surroundings more diverse and should be protected."

A spokeswoman in Gore's office, realizing they had laid an egg on the Eagle letter, explained, "We get a lot of mail. This was an innocent mistake, and as soon as the Vice President heard about it, he wrote back the person to apologize and respond."

I wonder, when Al Gore was asked if he could do anything about the train dilemma, if he chanted "I think I can, I think I can, I think I can."

According to a poll conducted in 1975 by the
Madame Tussaud Waxworks in London, the most hated
men in history (past and present) were, in order:
Adolf Hitler, Idi Amin, Count Dracula, Richard M. Nixon,
and Jack the Ripper.

Not Worth the Paper . . .

Fans of Ronald Reagan, watch out. If you've got an autograph of Ronny from his days as a movie star, it's probably a forgery. According to autograph expert Herman Darvick, Reagan used to pay his mother Nelle seventy-five dollars a week to sign photographs and fan letters for him. And while you're at it, if you have any of Jane Wyman's autographs from the period when she was married to Ronald, look carefully. "She [Nelle] even signed Jane Wyman's name," warned Darvick.

"As to the Presidency, the two happiest days of my life were those of my entrance upon the office and my surrender of it." —Martin Van Buren

Why Not Leave Well Enough Alone!

Although it is well known that President James A. Garfield was assassinated, what isn't well known is that the assassin's bullet didn't kill him. President Garfield was shot by Charles J. Guiteau on July 1, 1881, but he didn't die until eighty days later, on September 19, 1881—of blood poisoning. Doctors believed it was best to remove the bullet from the president's back, and they continually dug around Garfield's wound with dirty instruments and unclean hands. Even Alexander Graham Bell got in on the action. He brought to the White House his newly invented metal detector. Using the new device was a great idea and probably would have worked perfectly—except for the fact that the president was lying on a metal bed. It is now believed that if the doctors hadn't tried to remove the bullet, the president would have made a full recovery.

John Kennedy, at age forty-three, was not the youngest man to become president. The youngest president was Theodore Roosevelt, at forty-two. Kennedy, however, was the youngest man to be elected president—Roosevelt became president when McKinley was assassinated.

The Assassination Nation—
Part II

All in all, eight presidents had their lives threatened by an assassin, not including presidential candidate George Wallace, who was shot May 15, 1972, and permanently crippled by Arthur Bremer. Here are the rest of the assassination attempts:

President Richard Nixon. February 22, 1974. Presidential-assassin-wanna-be Samuel Byck planned to kill Richard Nixon by hijacking a plane, shooting the pilot, then crashing the plane into the White House. He killed a Delta Airlines security guard and a copilot as the first phase of his assassination plot. But soon law enforcement agents began firing at Byck, he gave up his plot and, instead of surrendering to the authorities, shot himself in the head.

President Gerald Ford had the distinction of having two assassination attempts on his life. (Why anyone would want to kill Ford is beyond me.) The first took place on September 5, 1975, in Sacramento. Lynette "Squeaky" Fromme, a follower of Charles Manson, was disarmed by Secret Service agents before she could fire. The second attempt was on September 22, 1975, when an ex-marine, Oliver Sipple, tackled Sara Jane Moore just before she fired a shot—the bullet missed Ford. In both instances, Gerald Ford was completely unharmed.

President Ronald Reagan. March 30, 1981, in Washington, D.C. John W. Hinckley, Jr., apparently trying to impress actress Jodie Foster, wounded the president, wounded Secret Service agent Timothy J. McCarthy, and permanently crippled presidential press secretary James Brady. Reagan was rushed to the hospital where the bullet was removed and where he made a full recovery.

President Bill Clinton. October 29, 1994, in Washington, D.C. On the sidewalk outside the White House, Francisco Duran shot at a tourist who resembled the President. The real President was unharmed.

The father of our country, George Washington, never fathered a child. (His wife had two children by a previous marriage—whom Washington adopted.)

Impeach Preserves

When one thinks about Richard Nixon, the word "impeachment" comes to mind. However, Richard Nixon was never impeached—he resigned before Congress had a chance to kick him out. Andrew Johnson and Bill Clinton have the glory of being the only presidents against whom the Articles of Impeachment have been drawn. However, neither man was removed from office; both were found not guilty. There has never been a president removed from office by the vote of Congress. But there have been several cases throughout history when resolutions have been introduced into Congress to begin the impeachment process. Those presidents who were possible candidates for impeachment are:

John Tyler	Andrew Johnson	Grover Cleveland
Herbert Hoover	Harry Truman	Richard Nixon

Andrew Johnson came the closest to being removed from office—he was saved by a single vote.

**As a youngster, Ulysses S. Grant was given
the nickname "Useless Grant."**

Hickory Dickory

Andrew Jackson, known as "Old Hickory," was taunted into a duel by twenty-five-year-old Charles Dickinson of Nashville, Tennessee. The real reason Dickinson wanted to fight Jackson may never become known—but the excuse given was that Dickinson was fighting for the honor of a friend whom Jackson had caned. Using articles in the *Impartial Review,* Dickinson called Jackson "a poltroon, a coward, and a worthless scoundrel." He also mentioned the fact that Jackson's wife, Rachel, wasn't divorced when Jackson and she married—making Rachel guilty of adultery. That got him. "[Your insults against Rachel] must be noticed and treated with the respect due a gentleman, although in the present instance you do not merit it," wrote Jackson in his May 22, 1806, letter calling Dickinson out for a duel. Dickinson knew he had the upper hand in the duel; he was twelve years younger than Jackson and considered an expert with pistols. It was reported that Dickinson would practice by snap-firing at a string stretched twenty-four feet away. Things didn't look good for Jackson—in fact, Jackson didn't look so good himself. He was terribly thin. On the day of the duel, Jackson arrived wearing an overcoat that looked a size or two too big. They paced off the twenty-four feet, turned, and faced each other. The command of "Fire!" was called and Dickinson got off the first shot. Jackson winced in pain and put his left hand to his chest. He then raised his gun and aimed. "God in heaven!" Dickinson shouted. "Is it possible that I missed him?" He stepped toward Jackson and was immediately ordered back into position. Jackson re-aimed and slowly squeezed the trigger. The bullet struck Dickinson in the abdomen and passed through his body, killing him. It was then noticed that Jackson was standing in a pool of blood. He removed his coat and it was discovered that Dickinson's bullet had hit Jackson only a fraction of a distance from his heart. Dickinson's aim was perfect, but since Jackson was so thin and was wearing an oversized coat, Dickinson misjudged where Jackson's heart really lay. The doctors decided not to remove the bullet. And a good thing, too—remember what happened to President Garfield when the doctors got ahold of him?

Alan Seeger's "I Have a Rendezvous with Death" was one of John F. Kennedy's favorite poems.

Amending His Ways

Even though Abraham Lincoln is probably best known for freeing the slaves through the Emancipation Proclamation (which didn't really free the slaves; see page 75), he actually supported just the opposite. In 1861, Lincoln endorsed the Corwin Amendment. Simply put, if the amendment had been approved, the Constitution couldn't have been changed to make slavery illegal. The Corwin Amendment was ratified by Congress, and three states approved it—then the Civil War started, and the amendment was quickly forgotten. But had things been a little different, the Thirteenth Amendment to the Constitution, the one that abolished slavery, could easily have been the amendment that made abolishing slavery unconstitutional. Lincoln would have gone down in the history books as the president who made the federal government powerless to abolish slavery instead of "The Great Emancipator."

"[The U.S. Navy urgently] needs modern musicians."
—Democratic presidential candidate Michael Dukakis,
in 1988. He meant to say "munitions."

Film at 11

We've seen it over and over again: the grainy, colored, home movie of the assassination of President John Kennedy. It's been in magazines, movies, television shows—I'm surprised it's not on a T-shirt. It's become part of our national history and our national consciousness; it's what most people see in their minds when they think of that fateful day in Dallas. It even has a nickname—the Zapruder Film, named after Abraham Zapruder, the man who was innocently making a film of the president in the parade. It's got his name, it was shot on his camera, so it must be his film, right? Not according to the government. While the Zapruder family has maintained the copyright, the actual film (confiscated the day of the assassination), along with several copies made on November 22, 1963, have been held in cold storage at the National Archives. In 1997, a decision by the Kennedy Assassination Records Review Board ruled that on August 1, 1998, the film would become public property as an official "assassination record."

The family of the late Abraham Zapruder is considering litigation that would invoke their constitutional right to "just compensation." And just what compensation are they asking for the film? Eighteen million dollars. The government wants to pay them only $750,000, however. The Zapruder family has hired President Clinton's private attorney Robert Bennett to begin negotiations with the government.

"That's a good question. Let me try to evade you."
—Paul Tsongas, presidential candidate in 1992,
responding to the question of whether he was
working to help Democratic nominee Bill Clinton or
working to further his own policies

A Dark Horse Candidate

"Here lies the body of my good horse, 'The General.' For twenty years he bore me around the circuit of my practice, and in all that time he never made a blunder. Would that his master could say the same!" —Inscription on the grave of President John Tyler's horse

As a young man, Rutherford B. Hayes fought lyssophobia—the fear of going insane.

The Presidential Look

The big question in most people's minds when Gerald Ford was chosen by Nixon to replace Spiro Agnew was "Who is this guy? What's he done before?" Well, among other things, Gerald Ford, as a young man, appeared in a 1939 edition of *Look* magazine with his girlfriend Phyllis Brown. It was an article about a weekend in the life of the "beautiful people." He later appeared on the cover of *Cosmopolitan.* Seems to make him as qualified to be president as nearly anyone else.

"I admire Ted Kennedy. How many fifty-nine-year-olds do you know who still go to Florida for spring break?"
—Patrick Buchanan, 1996 Republican
presidential hopeful

Iron Ron Reagan

Ronald Reagan is considered by many to have had the most "presidential" look. He looked like a president. But in 1940 Ronny must have looked buff because he was the winner of the University of California's "The Most Nearly Perfect Male Figure." And you thought Ford was a sexy guy.

"If you have a mother-in-law with only one eye and she has it in the center of her forehead, you don't keep her in the living room." —President Lyndon Baines Johnson, on why he wouldn't discuss America's military involvement in Vietnam

A Featherweight President

President Millard Fillmore actually signed a treaty about bird droppings. It was an agreement between the United States and Peru concerning bird poop, which has a high nitrate content and is an essential element used in making explosives and fertilizer. And scholars try to say that Millard Fillmore's presidency didn't accomplish much! That's pure crap!

"There's no difference between me and the president on taxes. No more nit-picking. Zip-a-dee-doo-dah. Now it's off to the races." —Vice President George Bush on his similarities to President Ronald Reagan

The Story of the Owl
and the Loon

In September 1996, Reform Party presidential candidate Ross Perot shared his thoughts on the conservation of the spotted owl. The survival of the spotted owl is thought to be threatened by the logging of mature trees in the Pacific Northwest. Perot came up with a way to make everybody happy.

"I was up in Washington state and the people were so worried about this huge area [where] they wouldn't let them do any timber cutting because of these owls, and I finally asked a relevant question," Perot said. "I said, 'How many owls are there?' They said 'twenty,' and I said, 'Okay, I suggest we send *Air Force One* out there, transport 'em in absolutely first-class comfort to the nearest national park. Now the owls can live happily ever after in hundreds of thousands of acres in some nearby park, [and] we can go back to work here.' "

"Whenever a man has cast a longing eye on offices, a rottenness begins in his conduct." —Thomas Jefferson

Grin and Bear It

At the battle of Vicksburg, during the Civil War, a servant girl accidentally poured out into the Mississippi River the water in a basin containing Ulysses S. Grant's false teeth. He was unable to eat solid food for a week until a dentist came and made him a new set of choppers.

According to experts, the value of a Michael Dukakis signature before he ran for president was $15; while he was running the value climbed to $100; after he lost, it dropped to $10.

Receiving Line or Punch Line?

One of the duties of the U.S. president is to greet and make small talk with huge crowds of people in receiving lines. At one such gathering, President Franklin Delano Roosevelt became bored with exchanging little pleasantries. He didn't think anyone was paying attention to what he said anyway. So to prove his point, as he took each patron's hand, he said, "I murdered my grandmother this morning." Most people smiled at the president and moved on. Only one man actually listened to what Roosevelt was saying and quickly responded, "She certainly had it coming!"

In 1850, former President John Tyler was so strapped for cash he was unable to pay a bill for $1.25 until he sold his corn crop for the year.

Dream a Little Dream of Me

President Lincoln had an envelope labeled "assassination" that contained more than eighty death threats he had received since taking office. He claimed the letters didn't cause him any concern because he never dreamed anyone would actually assassinate him—until he really did dream it. In early April 1865, Lincoln told his wife, Mary Todd, and his Illinois law partner, Ward H. Lamon, about an "amazingly real" dream "of the most startling import." Lamon recalled the telling of the dream in detail. The president had worked late into the evening and, when he went to bed, had fallen asleep quickly. In his dream everything was deathly still and he heard the pitiful sounds of many people crying in the distance. After walking from room to room in the White House, Lincoln finally came upon the crowd of mourning people gathered in the East Room.

"Before me was a catafalque [the raised structure on which a coffin rests during a state funeral]," Lincoln told his wife and Lamon. Many "were weeping pitifully." He asked a soldier, "Who is dead in the White House?" The soldier answered, "The President. He was killed by an assassin!" Suddenly, the crowd wailed in unison and the noise caused Lincoln to awaken from his dream. "I slept no more that night; and although it was only a dream, I have been strangely annoyed by it ever since," he said. Mrs. Lincoln said she did not believe in such superstitious nonsense as a prophesy in a dream. But on Good Friday, April 14, just a few days after Lincoln confessed his dream, he and his wife were seated together watching a play at Ford's Theater.

The Battle of New Orleans, in which General Andrew Jackson successfully defeated the British (which made Jackson a national hero and later a president), was fought fifteen days after the War of 1812 had ended. Word of the war's end was late getting to Jackson.

Together Again

Richard Wilson paid $3,450 at the 1998 auction of Kennedy memorabilia for a pair of JFK's longjohns. Mr. Wilson plans to exhibit the underwear next to a slip and pair of panties formerly owned by Marilyn Monroe.

"Never kick a fresh turd on a hot day."
—Harry S Truman

Just Slipped His Mind

Thomas Jefferson penned his own epitaph before his death. It reads: "Here was buried Thomas Jefferson, author of the Declaration of Independence, of the Statute of Virginia for Religious Freedom, and father of the University of Virginia."

You'll notice Jefferson's oversight—he neglected to mention he had ever been the president of the United States.

"You know, your nose looks just like Danny Thomas's."
—President Ronald Reagan, during the Middle East
conflict, to the Lebanese foreign minister

All the Way with LBJ

"The difference between being a member of the Senate and a member of the House is the difference between chicken salad and chicken shit." —The answer given to then congressman George Bush by President Lyndon B. Johnson to the question of whether he should run for the Senate. Bush took Johnson's advice, ran for the Senate, and lost.

After leaving office President Calvin Coolidge went on to write a nationally syndicated newspaper column.

Memories—At the
Corners of My Eyes

In the 1995 Grammy Music Awards program there was a special tribute to Barbra Streisand written by President Bill Clinton. The article included the President's name and even a photograph. But before the program went to print, the White House decided to append a line at the bottom of the tribute that read, "Bill Clinton is President of the United States." I guess they wanted to make sure people wouldn't think it was written by Bill Clinton the saxophone player.

**"Being president is like being a jackass in a hailstorm.
There's nothing to do but to stand there and take it."
—Lyndon B. Johnson**

Quayle Quotes

Harry S Truman proclaimed "The vice presidency is about as useful as a cow's fifth teat," and J. Danforth Quayle (vice president under George Bush—1988–1992) has become the utter epitome of that statement, at least when it comes to misstatements.

Quotes from Dan Quayle:

"If we don't succeed, we run the risk of failure."

"Republicans understand the importance of bondage between a mother and child."

"The Holocaust was an obscene period in our nation's history. I mean in this century's history. But we all lived in this century. I didn't live in this century."

"When I have been asked during these last weeks who caused the riots and the killing in L.A., my answer has been direct and simple: Who is to blame for the riots? The rioters are to blame. Who is to blame for the killings? The killers are to blame."

"Quite frankly, teachers are the only profession that teach our children."

"I stand by all the misstatements that I've made."

Phil Gramm's 1996 presidential campaign staff sent out flyers detailing the "ethical problems" of opponent Lamar Alexander, including "incidents such as pelting out-of-state cars with snowballs [which] earned Alexander at least two paddlings in school."

Real
Yankee Doodle Dandies

Three presidents died on July 4—Thomas Jefferson and John Adams (both 1826) and James Monroe (1831). Jefferson and Adams were the only two signers of the Declaration of Independence to become president—they died on the fiftieth anniversary of the document's signing. Calvin Coolidge is the only president to have been born on the Fourth of July (1872).

In his youth, Ronald Reagan was awarded a ten-dollar tip for diving into the Rock River in Illinois and retrieving a swimmer's lost false teeth.

The First Real
American President

The first president to be born a citizen of the United States was the eighth president, Martin Van Buren. He was born on December 5, 1782, six years after the signing of the Constitution. Since all previous presidents had been born before the American Revolution, they were actually British subjects.

Thomas Jefferson wrote the Declaration of Independence in just eighteen days.

Fillmore or Less

"I had not the advantage of a classical education, and no man should, in my judgment, accept a degree he cannot read." —Millard Fillmore declining an honorary degree, with portions written in Latin, from Oxford University. Fillmore first attended school at age eighteen, surrounded by seven- and eight-year-olds. He became an excellent student and went on to marry his teacher, Abigail Powers, seven years later.

John F. Kennedy was such a skinny little boy that fellow schoolmates at Choate prep school called him "rat face."

More Quayle Quotes

I just couldn't help myself—there were too many for just one page! Actual quotes from Vice President Dan Quayle:

"We are ready for any unforeseen event that may or may not occur."

"For NASA, space is still a high priority."

"I am not part of the problem. I am a Republican."

"Mars is essentially in the same orbit. . . . Mars is somewhat the same distance from the Sun, which is very important. We have seen pictures where there are canals, we believe, and water. If there is water, that means there is oxygen. If oxygen, that means we can breathe."

"I love California, I practically grew up in Phoenix."

"A low voter turnout is an indication of fewer people going to the polls."

"It isn't pollution that's harming the environment. It's the impurities in our air and water that are doing it."

"Public speaking is very easy."

"I wish to see this beverage become common instead of the whiskey which kills one-third of our citizens and ruins their families." —Thomas Jefferson on beer

Still Getting Lost
in the Translation

In 1977, President Jimmy Carter visited Poland. Since he didn't speak the language, he brought along a translator. But, if one doesn't speak a foreign language, one is never sure what the interpreter is actually saying. When Carter said to a gathering of officials and the press corps that he had "left the United States that day," his interpreter said he'd "abandoned" it. Carter made reference to the Poles' "desires for the future." His interpreter translated this as "lusts for the future." And, to top it all off, the interpreter explained to the confused but possibly aroused crowd: "The President says he is pleased to be here in Poland grasping your private parts." If Carter had spoken to American voters that way he may have won a second term.

During the 1984 presidential election, the residents of Midland, Pennsylvania, were offered $3 million by Saudi Sheik Mohammed al-Fassi if they would pledge not to vote for Ronald Reagan.

Bite My Lips

"While the press is here, was there—did the Democratic governors meet, and is there any feeling that we shouldn't press to try to get something done by March 20th? Do we—is there—can anyone—is there a spokesman on this point? Because what I would like to suggest—not that you have to sign every 't' and 'l' but that we urge Congress to move by that date. And if that date isn't good, what date? Is there a feeling on that one?" —President George Bush in a speech to the National Governor's Association, February 3, 1992

Warren G. Harding and John F. Kennedy were the only presidents to have been survived by their fathers.

Brand Names

Most people are stuck with the name they are given at birth—unless, of course, they legally change it. However, in the history of the United States, there have been five presidents who altered their names—just a little. Ulysses S. Grant was born Hiram Ulysses Grant and had his name changed accidentally by the army. Grover Cleveland's real name was Stephen Grover Cleveland (which has a nice ring to it), but he decided to drop his first name, as did Thomas Woodrow Wilson and John Calvin Coolidge. Dwight David Eisenhower's real name was David Dwight Eisenhower—he didn't like the order and reversed his first and middle name. There are also four presidents who are known by their initials: Franklin Delano Roosevelt (FDR), John Fitzgerald Kennedy (JFK), Lyndon Baines Johnson (LBJ), and Theodore Roosevelt, who hated the nickname "Teddy" and preferred "TR."

**Thomas Jefferson, while serving in Congress, introduced
a bill that proposed barring slavery from any future
states admitted to the Union. This measure could
have prevented the Civil War had it not been
defeated—by a single vote.**

Secret Service
Slumber Party

The Secret Service is a group of highly trained, heavily armed men and women who, among their other duties, are sworn to protect the president of the United States. So no one would be dumb enough to try to rob a hotel filled with Secret Service agents, right? You'd be surprised. Three armed men confronted the night clerk at an AmeriSuites Hotel in Little Rock, Arkansas, apparently unaware the hotel was serving as a temporary dormitory for Secret Service agents assigned to protect President Clinton and Vice President Gore. One agent who saw the holdup gave chase to the gunmen in a van and was soon joined by other agents. Two of the three gunmen were shot in their getaway car. "Didn't they think anything was unusual when they saw the parking lot?" mused one agent, explaining that the hotel parking lot was jammed with Chryslers, Jeep Cherokees, and unmarked vans, all bearing District of Columbia license plates and prominently exposed emergency lights in their grillwork.

At age forty-nine, James Knox Polk was the youngest president until Theodore Roosevelt, and he worked twelve to fourteen hours a day, seven days a week. He literally died from exhaustion only three months after leaving the White House.

The Long and Short of It

William Henry Harrison was sixty-nine years old when he was elected president. Up until that time he was the oldest president ever to take office. (Reagan, at sixty-nine years 349 days, then reelected at seventy-three, beat Harrison's record.) Harrison is generally known for three things—one, his age. Two, he gave the longest inaugural address in United States history—8,445 words lasting one hour and forty minutes. Three, he served the shortest time in office—thirty-two days. And the three are related. Trying to prove his age wasn't a factor, Harrison rode horseback through the long inaugural parade and then gave his lengthy speech outside in the brisk March wind without a hat, coat, or gloves. He caught a cold that turned into pneumonia and killed him. In fact, the president died so soon after being elected that his wife, who stayed in Ohio to prepare for the move to Washington, never had a chance to move into the White House. An interesting footnote is that even though Harrison's speech was the longest in American history, it had originally been longer—it was edited by Daniel Webster.

"I was not lying. I said things that later on seemed to be untrue." —Richard M. Nixon, during a 1978 interview concerning Watergate

Alexander's Rotten, Horrible, No Good, Very Bad Day

When Lamar Alexander was running in the Republican presidential primary in 1996, he was asked a very interesting question by a reporter during a stop in New Hampshire. While President Clinton was being asked about his liaisons and Whitewater, and Bob Dole was being asked about his physical well-being, Lamar was asked about groceries. One reporter at a news conference asked Alexander if he could tell the audience the price of a dozen eggs and a gallon of milk. Alexander didn't answer the reporter's question and quickly ended the press conference. He then spun around and said to an aide standing nearby, "I need to know the price of a gallon of milk and a dozen eggs—now. I need to know right now."

After Independent presidential candidate Ross Perot pulled out of the race in 1992, disenchanted Perot supporters were known to have moved their "Run, Ross, Run" bumper stickers from the back of their cars to their front bumpers.

Happy Birthday
to . . . Who?

There have been a lot of stories mentioned in this book that dispel popular myths about our presidents—it seems as if nothing we learned in history classes was correct. But one thing is certain: George Washington was born on February 22—Washington's Birthday. Not so. In fact, Washington was actually born on February 12—Lincoln's birthday (which didn't bother Abe since he wasn't born yet). What happened was, in 1732, when Washington was born, America, which was still a colony of Great Britain, was on the Julian calendar. When George turned twenty, however, it was decided that the Gregorian calendar would be used from then on. So that changed Washington's birthday from February 12 to February 22, a change that surely must have confused young George. It's a good thing Washington isn't alive today—apart from being nearly 270 years old, he would have to celebrate his birthday, regardless of the actual date, on whichever Monday came the closest.

Before Dwight D. Eisenhower, the presidential retreat was called Shangri-La, after the mountain settlement in James Hilton's novel *Lost Horizon.* Eisenhower thought the name sounded too snotty and renamed the retreat Camp David in honor of his grandson.

Madam President

There's been talk of a woman running for president for many years now—but not much talk about the woman president we already had. I'm talking about Edith Bolling Galt Wilson, the wife of Woodrow Wilson. On September 26, 1919, President Woodrow Wilson had a nervous breakdown that was followed on October 2, 1919, by a severe stroke. Edith Wilson had her husband placed in seclusion, and she, and she alone, decided whom the president could see and, amazingly enough, what legislation from Congress would get into his hands. The severity of the president's illness was kept a secret and therefore, the authority of the president wasn't passed on to the vice president. The president was paralyzed on the left side so it was Edith Wilson who actually signed the president's name to a number of documents. As she explained, "I studied every paper sent from the different Secretaries or Senators, and tried to digest and present in tabloid form the things that, despite my vigilance, had to go to the President. I, myself, never made a single decision regarding the disposition of public affairs. The only decision of mine was what was important and what was not, and the very important decision of when to present matters to my husband."

One person Mrs. Wilson decided shouldn't bother the president was Thomas R. Marshall, Wilson's vice president, who was turned away from the White House without an explanation. Deciding that the president was incapable of carrying out his duties and the fact that the vice president wasn't in the White House, Secretary of State Alexander Haig . . . uh, I mean, Secretary of State Robert Laning claimed "I'm in charge now" and called a Cabinet meeting. Mrs. Wilson was incensed at Laning's assumption of power and demanded his resignation.

And she got it. She then, with the president's blessing, of course, assigned Bainbridge Colby the position of Secretary of State even though Colby had no experience in foreign affairs. Wilson recuperated from his stroke and slowly regained control of the White House.

George Herbert Walker Bush is the only president with four names.

Not Gonna Do It!

"The idea that I should become President seems to me too visionary to require a serious answer. It has never entered my head, nor is it likely to enter the head of any other person." —Zachary Taylor two years prior to his victory in being elected the twelfth president of the United States

Richard M. Nixon is the only president to have won an Emmy award. He received the Best Spoken Word award for an album made from the soundtrack of his television interview with David Frost.

Suffering Suffragette

There are two women who ran for president and shared a very unusual situation in history. Even though they ran for the office, they couldn't vote for themselves, or anyone else for that matter. Victoria Claflin Woodhull ran on the National Radical Reform ticket in 1872 and Belva Ann Bennett Lockwood ran on the National Equal Rights ticket in both 1884 and 1888. Why could they run for the presidency but not vote in the election? Because both women ran before the Nineteenth Amendment to the Constitution was ratified in 1920—giving women the right to vote.

"I am like the man who was tarred and feathered and ridden out of town on a rail. When they asked him how he felt about it, he said that if it were not for the honor of the thing, he would rather have walked."
—President Abraham Lincoln

Ranking the Presidents

In 1997, Ridings-McIver, a professional polling company, polled 719 historians and former politicians who ranked the forty-one presidents on the basis of five factors: leadership qualities, accomplishments and crisis management, political skill, political appointments, and character and integrity. May I have the envelope, please.

1. Abraham Lincoln
2. Franklin Roosevelt
3. George Washington
4. Thomas Jefferson
5. Theodore Roosevelt
6. Woodrow Wilson
7. Harry Truman
8. Andrew Jackson
9. Dwight Eisenhower
10. James Madison
11. James Polk
12. Lyndon Johnson
13. James Monroe
14. John Adams
15. John Kennedy
16. Grover Cleveland
17. William McKinley
18. John Quincy Adams
19. Jimmy Carter
20. William Howard Taft
21. Martin Van Buren
22. George Bush
23. Bill Clinton
24. Herbert Hoover
25. Rutherford Hayes
26. Ronald Reagan
27. Gerald Ford
28. Chester Arthur
29. Zachary Taylor
30. James Garfield
31. Benjamin Harrison
32. Richard Nixon
33. Calvin Coolidge
34. John Tyler

35. William Henry Harrison
36. Millard Fillmore
37. Franklin Pierce
38. Ulysses Grant

39. Andrew Johnson
40. James Buchanan
41. Warren Harding

"Wherever I have gone in this country, I have found Americans." —Alfred M. Landon (Republican), while campaigning in America against Franklin D. Roosevelt in 1936. Landon's claim to fame came when Roosevelt beat him with 523 electoral votes to 8, the biggest defeat in American history.

A Cure for What Ails You

"Since I came to the White House, I got two hearing aids, a colon operation, skin cancer, a prostate operation, and I was shot. The damn thing is I've never felt better in my life." —President Ronald Reagan in 1987

While finishing his coffee at the Maxwell House Hotel, President Theodore Roosevelt commented, "It's good to the last drop." The remark became Maxwell House's slogan from that time on.

Rank and File

During the same poll, Ridings-McIver selected "Character and Integrity" as a separate factor and polled only on that trait. The presidents ranked a little differently. I know you're going to do it anyway—so go ahead and skip to the end of the list!

1. Abraham Lincoln
2. George Washington
3. John Adams
4. John Quincy Adams
5. Jimmy Carter
6. James Madison
7. Thomas Jefferson
8. Woodrow Wilson
9. Harry Truman
10. Dwight Eisenhower
11. Herbert Hoover
12. Theodore Roosevelt
13. James Monroe
14. William Howard Taft
15. Franklin Roosevelt
16. Grover Cleveland
17. Gerald Ford
18. Andrew Jackson
19. William McKinley
20. James Polk
21. Calvin Coolidge
22. Rutherford Hayes
23. Zachary Taylor
24. George Bush
25. Martin Van Buren
26. James Garfield
27. John Tyler
28. Benjamin Harrison
29. William Henry Harrison
30. Andrew Johnson
31. Millard Fillmore
32. Ulysses Grant
33. Chester Arthur
34. John Kennedy
35. Franklin Pierce
36. James Buchanan

37. Lyndon Johnson

38. Bill Clinton

39. Ronald Reagan

40. Warren Harding

41. Richard Nixon

"Trees cause more pollution than automobiles."
—Ronald Reagan in 1981

A Story You Can Sink Your Teeth Into

The things we associate with George Washington are: He chopped down the cherry tree (which he didn't), he threw a silver dollar across the Potomac River (which he didn't; silver dollars weren't minted until four years before Washington's death—and besides, it would take a cannon to shoot a coin across the wide banks of the Potomac), and his dentures were made out of wood (which also isn't true). Washington's dentures were, in fact, made out of hippopotamus ivory. A New York City dentist, John Greenwood, made President Washington several sets of dentures. Greenwood tried for years to save the last remaining tooth Washington had (the first bicuspid in his left lower jaw). In 1789, Greenwood made Washington's first set of dentures out of human teeth (not Washington's) fastened with gold rivets, with the remainder made of hippo ivory. Sadly, Greenwood had to extract the president's last remaining tooth in 1796; he had it encased in a gold locket and inscribed: "In New York 1790. Jn Greenwood made Pres Geo Washington a whole sett of teeth. The enclosed tooth is the last one which grew in his head." Wow, some people will keep anything.

"I don't suppose there's any public figure that's ever been subject to any more violent personal attacks than I have." —Bill Clinton

Missed Him by That Much

Duels were a big thing in the nineteenth century—President Andrew Jackson took place in a duel and won; Alexander Hamilton took place in a duel and lost. It has been believed for a number of years that Alexander Hamilton was too decent a man to actually shoot Vice President Aaron Burr in 1804 and that he purposely fired into the air instead of trying to kill the VP. The VP, on the other hand, took steady aim after Hamilton's miss and shot the man on the ten-dollar bill dead. Turns out that's not exactly how it happened. It seems Hamilton was trying to use an unfair advantage which, if I may say, backfired on him. During the bicentennial celebration in 1976, the Smithsonian Institution thought it would be a good idea to restore the pistols used in the Burr-Hamilton duel to their original condition. When they started the restoration process they discovered that the pistols—both supplied by Hamilton—had several features not allowed on dueling pistols . . . most important, a special hair-trigger feature. Being that they were both Hamilton's guns, it is believed that Hamilton utilized this illegal feature and set the trigger on his gun to require only a half pound of pressure to fire. The other gun was set at the normal, non-hair-trigger setting, which required ten to twelve pounds of pressure to fire. In a duel both men lower their guns and fire at the same time—the less pressure it takes to fire the gun, the quicker the gun can be fired. So Hamilton wasn't a kind, generous, caring individual who purposely missed so as not to take the life of a fellow human being. What really happened was that Hamilton, nervous over the fact that he was involved in a duel or the fact that he knew he had a special advantage over his opponent, held his gun too tightly and accidentally fired into the leaves above Burr's head.

"I may be President of the United States, but my private life is nobody's damned business." —Chester Alan Arthur

Nixon's the One!

Here's one you might find hard to swallow—Nixon wasn't as conservative as most people believe. Take one look at photographs of Nixon and he would seem the perfect poster child for a conservative, right-wing president. But he wasn't—in fact, he was pretty darn liberal if you look at the legislation he passed.

- He established the Environmental Protection Agency, the Occupational Safety and Health Administration, the Legal Services Administration, and the Equal Opportunity Commission.
- He opened diplomatic relations with Communist China.
- He more than doubled funding for the National Endowment of the Arts and National Endowment of Humanities.
- He greatly expanded the food-stamp program.
- Nixon's Philadelphia Plan of 1970 set up timetables and goals and incorporated government-mandated racial quotas. The plan also extended civil rights legislation to women.
- He was a staunch supporter of the Equal Rights Amendment.
- He proposed a national health insurance plan—which was rejected by Congress (which was then made up of a majority of Democrats) because they believed it didn't stretch far enough.
- His Family Assistance Plan would have initiated a guaranteed annual income for poor families and given assistance to three times as many children as then covered by Aid for Families with Dependent Children payments.

Most political analysts agree that, judged solely on the legislation he sponsored, Nixon would be considered the third most liberal president the United States has ever had; Franklin D. Roosevelt and Lyndon Johnson were first and second, respectively. Carter, Kennedy, and Clinton may have given the appearance of being superliberals but got far less liberal legislation enacted.

"In a very Christian way, as far as I'm concerned, he can go to hell." —Jimmy Carter of the Reverend Jerry Falwell

Think Pink

Wanting to tread the politically correct path, President Clinton set up a meeting with nearly forty elected homosexual officials to get information and ascertain concerns involving his administration and the gay community. White House guards were stationed and formally greeted the various gay state senators, representatives, city council members, judges, etc. with one unauthorized uniform accessory—they wore rubber gloves. Most of the gay officials were insulted by the protective hand-wear. Mike Nelson, an alderman from Carrboro, North Carolina, said he was "offended and disappointed" by the assumption "that everyone who is gay had AIDS." I wonder if the guards thought that's what the song meant by "don we now our gay apparel."

"Mothers all want their sons to grow up to be president, but they don't want them to become politicians in the process." —John F. Kennedy

But How Do You
Really Feel?

Not everyone has nice things to say about former presidents—not even former presidents.

"Richard Nixon is a no-good lying bastard. He can lie out of both sides of his mouth at the same time and if he ever caught himself telling the truth, he'd lie just to keep his hand in."
—Harry S Truman on President Richard Milhous Nixon

Woodrow Wilson once referred to President Chester A. Arthur as "a nonentity with side whiskers."

"McKinley has no more backbone than a chocolate eclair."
—Theodore Roosevelt's opinion of President William McKinley
(1898, regarding the Spanish-American War)

"Gerry Ford is so dumb he can't fart and chew gum at the same time."
—Lyndon Johnson on then Republican Minority Leader, and future president, Gerald Ford

"It is said he is a disgusting man to do business. Coarse, dirty, and clownish in his address and stiff and abstracted in his opinions, which are drawn from books exclusively."
—William Henry Harrison on John Quincy Adams

President James Garfield had the ability to simultaneously write Latin with one hand and Greek with the other.

Better Late than Never

The Federal Election Commission is supposed to oversee political contributions and prosecute when violations have taken place. So in 1988 when information about suspicious contributions to the Bush campaign surfaced, the FEC got right on it. A short seven years later, in December 1995, they had drawn their conclusion: The Bush campaign had received $223,000 in illegal contributions (from the National Republican Committee and several state parties used to pay for sixteen trips). There was one problem—Bush wasn't president in 1995. So, to show they meant business, the FEC sent a letter to the campaign's lawyers warning them to "take steps to ensure that this kind of activity does not occur in the future." Actually, the voters had already taken steps to make sure it didn't happen again—they'd voted for someone else.

F.D. ROOSEVELT

"These Republican leaders have not been content with attacks upon me, or on my wife, or on my sons—no, not content with that, they now include my little dog, Fala. Unlike the members of my family, he resents this."
—Franklin Delano Roosevelt

A Miss and Andy

President Andrew Jackson was walking down the steps of the U.S. Capitol on January 30, 1835, when suddenly Richard Lawrence, a house painter with a history of mental illness, rushed toward the president. Lawrence reached into his waistcoat and pulled out a single-shot derringer. Before the president could react, Lawrence took aim and pulled the trigger. The percussion cap exploded but for some reason the gunpowder in the barrel failed to ignite. Jackson was furious with the attempt on his life and raised his cane to strike the would-be assassin. Lawrence was quicker than Old Hickory, however, and deftly pulled out another single-shot derringer and fired at the president, now standing less than four feet away. The percussion cap exploded with a pop but again the gunpowder failed to ignite. Lawrence was captured and taken to jail. The president escaped the assassination attempt unharmed. The pistols were examined by weapons experts who concluded that both pistols were in working order—they both *should* have fired. The odds that two successive malfunctions on pistols of this sort would occur was calculated to be in the range of 125,000 to 1. Andrew Jackson lived another ten years and died quietly in his bed at the Hermitage in Nashville, Tennessee, at age seventy-eight.

Lyndon Baines Johnson was in the habit of conducting meetings while sitting on the toilet.

Give 'Em Hell, Harry!

"The people can never understand why the President does not use his supposedly great power to make 'em behave. Well, all the President is, is a glorified public relations man who spends his time flattering, kissing and kicking people to get them to do what they are supposed to do anyway." —President Harry Truman in a letter to his sister (1947)

"He is too immature to be entrusted with the leadership responsibilities inherent in sea duty." —Taken from a 1955 report concerning Ross Perot while he was serving in the U.S. Navy

A Mouse in the White House

It's been said before, and President Bill Clinton and VP Al Gore both agree, it's the computer age. That's why Bill and Al, along with twenty thousand volunteers, pledged to help three thousand California public schools hook up to the Internet. Clinton and Gore encouraged all schools to join the White House on the web, which would give them access to the vast resources on line. "What's our e-mail address, Al?" Clinton asked. "It's www dot whitehouse, one word, don't capitalize it, dot, 1600 Pennsylvania Avenue," Gore replied. Too bad the Vice President was way out in cyberspace on the address—which is actually "president@whitehouse.gov" and "vicepresident@whitehouse.gov." It's also the age of information—but let's get the right information, shall we?

"Hooters Welcomes President Clinton." —Sign outside a Rhode Island nightspot, known for its scantily clad waitresses, welcoming the President's motorcade

One More Time!

"No doubt about it," said U.S. Secretary of the Navy Thomas W. Gilmer, "our new cannon will be heard around the world." Gilmer's words would mean more than he could know. What he was talking about was the "Peacemaker," a super-cannon being test-fired on February 28, 1844, aboard the gunship *Princeton*. President John Tyler and four hundred dignitaries and guests had been invited by Captain Stockton to view the firing. The first two firings of the cannon were spectacular and everyone was pleased. The president, Captain Stockton, and guests then retired belowdecks for a banquet, several impromptu songs, and general merrymaking. Captain Stockton was barraged by requests for an additional firing of the cannon and, finally yielding to his guests, agreed. President Tyler signaled to Stockton that he would be there in a minute, and the captain and hundreds of guests went back above. Tyler's foot was on the bottom rung of the ladder leading to the deck when his son-in-law started singing a military song—the president thought it would be rude not to stop and listen. When William Waller finished his song he was met with a round of applause and the sound of the Peacemaker's final firing of the evening. Suddenly a commotion broke out and shouts of "Surgeons! All surgeons! To the deck at once." When Tyler arrived on deck he was met with a scene of total carnage. The breech of the huge, wrought-iron cannon had exploded and blasted jagged chunks of hot metal into the crowd. Navy Secretary Gilmer was dead, as was Secretary of State Abel P. Upshur, New York Senator David Gardiner, and Tyler's personal body slave, who was almost always at his side. Being the guest of honor Tyler would have been standing beside the huge cannon when it exploded and would have been instantly killed—but he was saved by a song. Tyler's political rival, James G. Bitney of the Liberty Party, wrote, "Many mourners marvel that President John Tyler was not among the dead. It is incredible that a jolly military song should have delivered this man from crippling injury or sudden death." The shock of the president's miraculous survival was soon overshadowed by the shock of his unexpected marriage just four months later. Tyler, who was then fifty-four, married Julia Gardiner, who was just twenty-four; she was also the daughter of the New York Senator who was killed when the cannon exploded.

**James K. Polk was the first full-term president
not to seek reelection.**

Garfield, the President— Not the Cat

"You may write down in your books now the largest percentage of blunders which you think I will be likely to make, and you will be sure to find in the end that I have made many more than you have calculated, many more." —A refreshingly honest and humble remark by James Garfield. Unfortunately, he was assassinated just four months into his presidency and unable to make all the blunders he had envisioned.

"I'm glad nobody found out about that manicure I got in California." —Bill Clinton in 1993, referring to the negative publicity over the $200 haircut he received on *Air Force One*

Johnny Rebel

John Tyler wasn't honored after his death on January 18, 1862, and no official word of his death was ever issued. Why? Because Tyler was considered a traitor in the North, even though he had been president of the United States. On May 5, 1861, Tyler accepted a seat in the provisional congress of the Confederate States of America. A few months later he was elected to represent his congressional district in the permanent C.S.A. Congress. Tyler was truly a rebel and the only president to ever hold office in the Confederacy. When he died he even had a Confederate flag, not an American flag, draped over his casket. It wasn't until fifty years after the Civil War ended, in 1915, that the United States finally erected a memorial stone over his grave.

"I don't necessarily consider McDonald's junk food. You know, they have chicken sandwiches, they have salads . . ." —Bill Clinton in 1993, defending his favorite fast-food chain

Strong as a Bull Moose

A crowd had gathered at a Milwaukee, Wisconsin, auditorium on October 14, 1912, to listen to a speech by Theodore Roosevelt, who was running for president on the Progressive Party (Bull Moose) ticket. While Roosevelt was preparing to give his speech, a man by the name of John Flammang Schrank shot him at a distance of six feet. The bullet hit Roosevelt in the chest and embedded itself in his fourth rib. Suddenly Progressive Party aide Henry Cochems announced to the crowd, "Ladies and gentlemen"—his voice broke—"I have something to tell you and I hope you will receive the news with calmness. Colonel Roosevelt has been shot!"

The news was so unbelievable that several people shouted out "Fake! Fake!" Theodore Roosevelt bounded onto the stage and pushed Cochems from the podium all the while undoing his coat. He dramatically opened one side to reveal the lower half of his shirt covered in blood. "I am going to ask you to be very quiet," bellowed TR. "If you'll do that, I will do the best I can . . ." Roosevelt's speech lasted for eighty minutes, and he gave a riveting oration only occasionally referring to his text. After the speech was over Roosevelt finally allowed himself to be taken to the hospital for X rays.

Dr. Alexander Lamber examined both the president's wound and the X ray and came to a startling conclusion. The president's life was saved because of his speech. Roosevelt had the entire three-hundred-page speech rolled in the breast pocket of his coat. The bullet passed through the manuscript before entering the president's body—which slowed it down tremendously. Lamber,

Roosevelt's family physician, said, "No doubt about it, his speech saved the Colonel's life." If Roosevelt had had a better memory, he probably would have died that day.

The three best-known Western names in China are Jesus Christ, Elvis Presley, and Richard Nixon.

Character Assassination

The four assassinated presidents and the six others whose lives were threatened by assassination had something to say about the matter—either before or after. Here's what three presidents had to say about assassins.

"If it is [God's] will that I must die at the hand of an assassin, I must be resigned. I must do my duty as I see it, and leave the rest with God."
—Abraham Lincoln (1864)

"I have no enemies. Why should I fear?"
—William McKinley on assassination

"He must have been crazy. None but an insane person could have done such a thing. What could he have wanted to shoot me for?"
—James A. Garfield on his deathbed

Thomas Jefferson and James Madison were both arrested in Vermont in the spring of 1791 for the crime of carriage-riding on a Sunday.

Speak Now or Forever Hold Your Peace

"If I am to speak ten minutes, I need a week for preparation; if fifteen minutes, three days; if half an hour, two days; if an hour, I am ready now."
—President Woodrow Wilson, known for his concise speeches, replying to the question of how long it took him to prepare his talks

Calvin Coolidge used to have his head rubbed with petroleum jelly while he ate breakfast in bed.

Making Waves

John Quincy Adams wasn't the most well-liked president. He was very stiff and unapproachable; and as the son of the second president, John Adams, John Quincy Adams considered himself close to royalty. He was also a sexist, refusing to give interviews to female reporters. He said he would, at convenient times, honor requests for interviews from male reporters, however. This infuriated Anne Royall. Ms. Royall was the widow of a Revolutionary War veteran and was left without a dime after her husband's death. In order to make ends meet she had taken up the relatively new-to-women field of journalism and wanted desperately to be the first woman to interview a president. John Quincy Adams's proclamation might have put an end to her dream if she wasn't so persistent. She became familiar with the president's schedule, especially the fact that he took a daily skinny-dipping session in the waters of the Potomac. Bathing suits hadn't been invented at that time—so this wasn't a particularly scandalous thing to do.

One morning Anne Royall walked up to the banks of the Potomac, pencil and paper in hand, and sat down on the president's clothes. The president, seeing no way out of the situation, or out of the water, told Ms. Royall he would give her the interview she requested at the executive mansion. But she knew a fox when she saw one—she refused to budge and told the president she wanted the interview right then and there. If he didn't cooperate, she threatened, she would scream and attract the attention of several fishermen downstream. A dripping wet, naked president and a screaming woman *would* be scandalous. So the president gave her the interview while standing in water up to his chin.

An eleven-year-old girl from Westfield, New York—
Grace Bedell—suggested to Abraham Lincoln that he
grow a beard. She said his face was too thin and
if he grew a beard more people would vote for him.
He did and she was right.

In the Line of Fire

Presidents have been forced to stand in receiving lines and shake hands with admiring crowds as part of their job for centuries. But what happened to William McKinley on the afternoon of September 6, 1901, changed how presidents deal with the public. While visiting the Pan-American Exposition at Buffalo, New York, William McKinley patiently greeted an enormous line of well-wishers who had come to meet the president at the Temple of Music. Waiting nervously in line was Leon F. Czolgosz, a Detroit native of Polish descent, who had his right hand wrapped in a bandage. McKinley, who always wore a red carnation in his lapel for good luck, spotted a young girl in the crowd and uncharacteristically removed his carnation and gave it to the girl. Czolgosz moved closer in line to McKinley, and when the president reached out his hand, Czolgosz fired two shots from a .32 Iver Johnson revolver concealed in the bandage. A button on McKinley's waistcoat deflected one of the bullets, but the other one hit the president in the abdomen. It passed through his stomach, grazing his left kidney, and came to rest in his pancreas. As he lay on the ground, McKinley said to a friend, "My wife," he whispered, "be careful, how you tell her—oh, be careful." Eight days later he was dead.

Valentine's Day, 1914, was the worst day in Theodore Roosevelt's life; his mother died of typhoid fever in the morning, and in the afternoon, his wife died giving birth to their daughter.

Lincoln's Log

President Lincoln has long been admired as being a great and fair president. However, during the Civil War, Lincoln did a few things that would be considered downright un-American. In 1861, the Lincoln administration not only censored the news but also closed down publication of the *New York News* for its anti-administration editorials. In 1863, they closed them down again for alleged spy activity. Lincoln liked a good joke—he could apparently dish it out—but he couldn't take it. When the *New York World* satirized Lincoln in 1863 he personally ordered the paper shut down and its editors arrested. How can anyone be expected to act civil during a war, anyhow?

"I just wanted to get a little attention." —George Bush, after vomiting on Japanese Prime Minister Kiichi Miyazawa

At No Time Did His Lips
Leave His Face

In March 1991, before a joint session of Congress, President George "Read My Lips" Bush said, "It would be tragic if the nations of the Middle East and the Persian Gulf were now, in the wake of the war, to embark on a new arms race."

Two months later, during a speech at the United States Air Force Academy, Bush said, "Nowhere are the dangers of weapons proliferation more urgent than in the Middle East." He then proclaimed, "I am today proposing a Middle East arms control initiative," which included "halting the proliferation of conventional and unconventional weapons in the Middle East." So there it was in plain English—putting a halt to the amount of weapons in the Middle East—so what happened next? President Bush, less than twenty-four hours later, announced plans to sell over $5 billion in new weapons to Bahrain, Egypt, Israel, Oman, Turkey, Saudi Arabia, and the United Arab Emirates.

He also had the Office of Munitions Control, the department responsible for monitoring arms sales to foreign countries, changed to the Center for Defense Trade. Two days later, Secretary Cheney, trying to explain the president's Doctor Jekyll/President Hyde turnabout said, "There is nothing inconsistent with on the one hand saying that we are interested in pursuing arms control and on the other hand providing for the legitimate security requirements that many of our friends in the region do have." Oh, now I understand!

"I have often thought that if there had been a good rap group around in those days, I would have chosen a career in music instead of politics." —Richard Nixon

An Affair to Remember

There's been a lot of talk recently about sexual indiscretions at the White House: the Bill Clinton/Paula Jones scandal, the Bill Clinton/Monica Lewinsky scandal, the John F. Kennedy/and nearly everybody scandal. But the presidential philandering didn't start there. Will the following presidents, who have cheated on their wives, please stand up: George Washington, James Garfield, Woodrow Wilson, Warren Harding, Franklin Delano Roosevelt, Lyndon Baines Johnson.

"That's got every fire hydrant in America worried."
—Bill Clinton on Dan Quayle's threatening to become
a "pit bull" in helping George Bush
regain the White House

Dick Dictates Dinner

Richard Milhous Nixon, to many, embodied the phrase "anal retentive." His too-tight suits, his sweaty upper lip, his forced smile all made up the Dick that he was. Here, in its entirety, is a memo to White House aide Rex Scouten dated July 9, 1969, that set out Nixon's rules for the serving order at state dinners.

1. If it is a stag dinner or lunch, with no guest of honor, the president will be served first.

2. If it is a stag affair, with a guest of honor, the guest of honor will be served first and the president next.

3. If it is a mixed dinner, with no guest of honor, Mrs. Nixon will be served first and the president next.

4. If it is a mixed dinner, with a guest of honor, the wife of the guest of honor will be served first simultaneously with Mrs. Nixon and then the guest of honor and I will be served second.

5. If it is one of those rare occasions where it is a mixed dinner and the guest of honor is not accompanied by his wife, serve Mrs. Nixon first and simultaneously the woman who is assigned as my dinner partner, and then serve me and the guest of honor second.

And if the president is caught engaging in illegal activities, he will be pardoned and everyone else in his cabinet will be served with a jail sentence.

"I strongly support the feeding of children."
—President Gerald Ford, discussing
the School Lunch Bill

Carter Uncovered

While researching his family history for a reunion in his hometown of Plains, Georgia, Jimmy Carter came to this conclusion: "Sometimes it's good not to know too much about your own family." Carter uncovered, among other things, that his great-great-grandfather, Wiley Carter, killed a man for stealing a slave. Carter's great-grandfather was shot to death in a gunfight in 1873 by his business partner. And in 1903, Carter's grandfather died after being shot in the back by a man who stole a table from the family store. "As far as I know," Carter said, "most of the other family members have been both law-abiding and peaceful in nature." Well, not quite; let's not forget Billy!

According to a survey conducted by the Pew Research Center, the words most commonly used to describe presidential candidate Ross Perot were: "Rich, crazy, idiot, egotistical, nuts, money, arrogant."

That's My Boy!!!

On July 21, 1884, the Buffalo *Evening Post* hit the stands with a story that was sure to destroy the career of Democratic presidential nominee Grover Cleveland. The story claimed that Grover was the father of an illegitimate boy named Oscar Folsom Cleveland. Allegedly, Grover had had an affair with a woman named Maria Halpin, as did several other Buffalo men in 1874, and the relationship resulted in the birth of a baby. Soon, the story of Grover's love child was on the newspaper wires appearing all across the United States. Grover looked doomed. Leaders of the Democratic Party wired Grover to ask what they should do about the situation: What spin should they take? Grover Cleveland sent back a message that to this day strikes fear in the heart of every politician; he said, "Tell the truth."

The truth was that Grover wasn't sure, nor was Maria Halpin, that the boy was actually his. It could have been any of the other men who routinely visited Maria, but Grover was the only bachelor. So to protect his married friends, Grover claimed responsibility and began financially supporting the child and the child's mother. When Maria became an alcoholic, Grover paid for her to be placed in an institution and the boy to be adopted by a well-to-do Buffalo family. When the "truth" came out, the public respected the way Grover had handled the situation. He hadn't lied. He hadn't blamed others. And he hadn't let anyone else take the fall. In fact, the public admired him so much on this issue that they elected him president over the opponent who had leaked the story, James G. Blaine.

"If you are sure you understand everything that is going on, you are hopelessly confused." —Walter Mondale

Dear John

"I have just received the following telegram from my generous Daddy. It says, 'Dear Jack: Don't buy a single vote more than is necessary. I'll be damned if I'm going to pay for a landslide.' " —John F. Kennedy joking about the rumor his father helped buy his election

"The voters have spoken—the bastards." —Morris Udall, expressing his feelings toward his 1976 loss in the presidential primary election

Infrequent Flyer

Would you like an all-expense-paid vacation to Moscow aboard *Air Force One*? Well, if not you, how about your luggage? When President Bill Clinton left a St. Petersburg hotel on his way to Moscow, his staff loaded up a pile of luggage from the lobby and put it aboard *Air Force One*. Seems the President's staff didn't read the tags on all the suitcases—one of them didn't belong to the President. It belonged to an Irish businessman who was identified only as "Kevin from Donegal." After some time the mistake was discovered, probably when the President tried to fit into the wrong-size underwear, and the luggage was returned. The President included a note of apology to Kevin, which read: "Sorry if we inconvenienced you. Your bags had a great tour of Moscow."

"I would have made a good pope." —Richard Nixon